P9-BIU-137

Table of Contents

Chapter 3: Taxation of a Limited Liability Company   39

Chapter 4: Limited Liability Legislation by State   51

Appendix: State Forms   127

Sample application forms demonstrate how to create
an LLC in the state of your choice.

Glossary   235

Index   241

Organization Forms

Preface

Since 1899, Corporate Agents, Inc., and its affiliated companies have helped businesspeople, lawyers, and accountants form corporations and limited liability companies legally, efficiently, and inexpensively. During this time, we have found that most people believe forming a corporation or a limited liability company is a formidable process which requires an attorney, extensive paperwork, and a great deal of time and money. It is not.

Our goal in writing *The Essential Limited Liability Company Handbook* is to show you how easy it is to form a limited liability company — commonly called an LLC. The mechanics of forming an LLC are simple and routine tasks that can be performed by anyone.

This book will help you gain an understanding of some of the basic legal and tax ramifications of various business structures. It will illustrate how the limited liability company structure compares to the more traditional forms of business organization.

In addition, this book provides detailed state-by-state LLC formation guidelines to help you prepare to file for limited liability company status. It explains exactly why corporate America looks so favorably on the Delaware LLC and why over 50 percent of the firms listed on the New York and American Stock Exchanges use Delaware as a resource for corporate services.

It is not the purpose of this guide to provide legal or tax advice. Before deciding to form a limited liability company, consult with an attorney or an accountant to determine if this business structure choice meets your needs.

Corporate Agents

Acknowledgment

Corporate Agents, Inc. would like to acknowledge Kevin J. Mirecki, Esq., the author of Chapter 3 on taxation, for his preparation and time and for the legal and financial advice he provided — Corporate Agents, Inc. does not offer legal or financial advice to our clientele.

Mirecki specializes in international law, estate planning, and asset protection. His law firm, with offices in Newport Beach and Los Angeles, is well known for its expertise in the development of the Asset Protection Planning Trust.

Chapter 1

Choosing a Limited Liability Company

A new business entity — the limited liability company, or LLC — has been created legislatively in all 50 states and in the District of Columbia. Hailed as the latest advance in the evolution of business formation in America, the LLC is actually not a new concept at all.

The first recognized limited liability company was formed in Germany in 1892. Limited liability companies quickly became the predominant form of business organization in many European and Latin American countries. In many instances, they have become more popular than corporations.

Wyoming wanted to capitalize on the benefits this business structure offered, particularly to small businesses. The state enacted the first U.S. LLC legislation, modeled after the German example, in 1977. Five years later, Florida followed Wyoming's lead. When the Internal Revenue Service passed Ruling 88-76 on September 2, 1988, other states also began to pass LLC legislation. The Wyoming law and the IRS ruling are the basis upon which most other state LLC regulations have since been drafted.

IRS regulations effective January 1, 1997, added flexibility to the LLC. This may have a significant role in your selection of the legal form of business you will choose when starting your new business. Limited liability companies that are properly formed in compliance with IRS regulations can offer individuals and small businesses a clear and, frequently, a superior alternative to general corporations, partnerships, and joint ventures. This is because the LLC combines the corporate advantage of limited personal liability with the pass-through tax advantage of partnerships. Many business advisers believe LLCs could ultimately replace general and limited partnerships, joint ventures, and general and S corporations. LLCs also offer definite advantages over sole proprietorships, and close or regular corporations with closely-held stock.

What is a Limited Liability Company?

The owners or shareholders of a LLC can be individuals, trusts, partnerships, corporations, and non-resident aliens. They can be active in the management of the business regardless of their share in the company. The LLC is a new statutory answer to at least three of the most pursued objectives of today's emerging entrepreneurs:

■ LLCs, like all types of corporations, offer limited personal liability — or simply limited liability — to its owners, called members. This means that their personal assets are protected from debts and lawsuits incurred by the business. In this case, owner liability is limited to the amount of the investment.

■ LLCs are treated like partnerships or S corporations for tax purposes. Business income, or loss, is only reported on the members' individual income tax return rather than on both the company and individual returns.

■ LLCs provide the most flexibility in business organization and management. In fact, many LLCs operate informally with little paperwork beyond a simple Operating Agreement or contract that describes a company's policies and organizational structure.

■ LLCs allow members to sell their interest without limitation or be subject to a right of first refusal by the other owners.

■ LLC managers need not own any interest in the LLC.

■ LLCs are not required to file for dissolution upon the death, bankruptcy, or insolvency of a member.

Deciding on a Business Structure

When you select the structure under which you will operate your business, you are making one of your most important business decisions. The basic organizational structures available to entrepreneurs today are sole proprietorships, partnerships, corporations, and limited liability companies.

The type of business organization you choose will depend on many factors, including: the nature of the business operation, legal restrictions, capital needs, tax advantages, intended division of earnings, number of owners, planned life of the business, and whether you need to protect personal assets from business debt.

The following comparisons of the advantages and disadvantages of limited liability companies vis-a-vis traditional business structures will help you clarify which organizational structure may best suit your situation.

LLC vs. Sole Proprietorship

A sole proprietorship is the simplest form of business organization and the most common type of business in America today. Simply put, a sole proprietorship is a business which is owned by one person. This can be the least costly and quickest way of starting a business because registering the business name and obtaining the necessary operating licenses may be all that is required.

Advantages of Sole Proprietorships

■ Easy to start.

■ Provide greatest freedom of action to follow your business vision.

■ You, the owner, make the business decisions.

■ Your business taxes are passed through to your personal IRS return.

Disadvantages of Sole Proprietorships

■ You, the owner, have unlimited personal liability for business debts. Personal and business obligations are one and the same.

- Illness or death may threaten your business.

- You are eligible for fewer business deductions compared to other types of business organizations.

When you own a sole proprietorship, you *are* the business. As a result, any debts or judgments against the business become your personal debts.

This means that your personal assets such as your home, car, and personal savings are exposed to business creditors. A limited liability company structure, on the other hand, separates your personal assets from your business assets. This usually gives business creditors recourse against your business assets only.

The pass-through tax advantage of passing business income through to your personal IRS return is the same for sole proprietorships and LLCs. However, fewer types of business deductions are allowed for sole proprietorships than for limited liability companies.

A sole proprietorship has only one major advantage over an LLC. It costs slightly less to form and to properly maintain than an LLC does.

LLC vs. Partnership

A partnership is a business structure with two or more owners. The two best known forms of partnerships are the general partnership and the limited partnership.

A general partnership can be formed with a simple oral agreement between two or more individuals. However, it is usually accomplished with a formal document known as a partnership agreement, drafted by an attorney to protect the partners' interest. Similar to sole proprietorships, your personal assets are not protected from creditors of your business.

Limited partnerships also involve two or more individuals. However, one of the partners — the limited partner — limits his or her activity in the business to capital investment. This partner does not actively participate in the management of the business. The other(s) — called general partners or operating partners — run the day-to-day operation of the business. Under this arrangement, the limited partner's personal liability for business debt is only as much as his or her capital investment. Unlike the operating partners, the limited partner's personal assets are not exposed.

In both general and limited partnerships, your taxes continue to pass through to your personal income statement. Unlike a sole proprietorship, you can obtain additional tax advantages by arranging income or loss to suit the needs of the individual parties. This can be done by modifying the percentage of the tax liability each partner is responsible for.

Advantages of Partnerships

- More individuals are needed to run the business.

- Additional sources of capital are required.

- There are more tax advantages through arrangement of profit or loss to suit the individual needs of the partners.

- More pass-through tax possibilities exist.

Disadvantages of Partnerships

- The personal assets of any operating partner are exposed to business creditors.

- Business is financially dependent on the limited partner in the case of limited partnerships.

- Illness or death may dissolve the business.

The limited liability company retains all the benefits of a partnership — especially pass-through tax treatment — while adding the advantage of limited liability protection.

An LLC is like a limited partnership because all of the LLC members have the same limited personal liability as the limited partner. An LLC is also like a general partnership because all the owners are free to participate in the management of the business. However, creating an LLC is more formal than the simple oral agreement of some partnerships, and involves an additional expense.

LLC vs. General Corporation

The general corporation is the most formal business structure available to business owners. It is a legal entity in its own right, separate from its owners, that is owned by an unlimited number of stockholders.

The owners' personal assets are protected from business creditors due to the legal separation of the corporation from the owners. Stockholders do not have liability for acts of the corporation and have financial exposure only to the limit of their investment.

Advantages of General Corporations

- Owners' personal assets are protected from business debt.

- The corporation has unlimited life that extends beyond the illness or death of the owners.

- A corporation receives tax-free benefits such as life and health insurance, travel and entertainment deductions, and retirement plans.

- Transfer of ownership is easily facilitated through the sale of stock.

- Change of ownership can occur without affecting management.

- It is easier to raise capital through the sale of stocks and bonds.

Disadvantages of General Corporations

- Corporations are more expensive to form than most other types of business.

- More legal formality and recordkeeping are required.

- More federal, state, and local rules and regulations affect the corporation.

Like general corporations, LLCs offer their owners protected personal liability from suits and judgments against the business. Unlike general corporations which have an unlimited lifespan, LLCs must set a predefined duration to keep the pass-through tax advantage. This is usually set at 30 years.

Under new tax laws effective January 1, 1997, a LLC is not required to file for dissolution in case of death, resignation, bankruptcy or insolvency of a member. In addition, any owner of interest in a LLC can sell their interest without limitation or be subject to a right of first refusal by the other members.

LLCs do not face double taxation like corporations. Instead, profit or losses are passed through directly to the owners of the limited liability company.

LLC vs. Close Corporation

There are two significant differences between general corporations and close corporations. First, most states that recognize close corporations limit ownership to 30 to 50 stockholders.

Second, and more importantly, ownership of a close corporation's stock is restricted. Sellers must offer corporate stock to existing owners before it is sold to new stockholders. The close corporation is particularly advantageous for the entrepreneur who wants to run a one-person corporation, or for the small group of individuals who all want to participate in running the business.

The similarities and differences between a close corporation and a LLC are much like those discussed with general corporations. Close corporations offer the same advantages as LLCs. On the downside, close corporation stock ownership restrictions can be very cumbersome. LLCs are not subjected to these same restrictions. Close corporations are double-taxed like general corporations.

LLC vs. S Corporation

S corporations have the same basic advantages and disadvantages as general and close corporations except that this corporate form allows stockholders to pass the profits or losses from the business directly to their personal income tax return. This eliminates the double taxation issue discussed above. However, in order to receive S corporation tax treatment by the IRS, the business owner(s) must first form a general or close corporation. Within 75 days of forming the corporation, all stockholders must elect the S corporation status by filing federal *Form 2553.*

S Corporation Requirements

Certain requirements must be met before qualifying for S corporation status. They are:

- The corporation must be a U.S. corporation.

- Only one class of stock is permitted.

- There can be only 75 stockholders.

- Only individuals may be stockholders. Other business entities cannot be stockholders.

- All stockholders must be U.S. citizens.

S corporations and LLCs are very similar. Both entities offer personal limited liability to the owners and solve the problem of double taxation. However, of the two, the LLC is the more accommodating business structure.

Advantages of LLCs Compared to S Corporations

Some of the advantages of incorporating as an LLC rather than an S Corporation for some companies are:

- LLCs allow unlimited ownership. S corporations are limited to an ownership of 75 persons.

- LLCs allow more than one class of stock.

- LLCs allow foreign ownership.

- LLCs allow ownership by other business entities as well as individuals.

Common Uses for the Limited Liability Company

It is not possible to adequately address all the ways a limited liability company may be used as a business structure here. Four entities which may particularly benefit from this organizational structure are highlighted below.

Family Business

There is no better form of family business ownership than the LLC. LLCs provide family businesses with pass-through tax treatment and limited liability protection without the ownership restrictions of its nearest business organizational rival — the S corporation. In addition, the LLC Operating Agreement is the most versatile document available. It enables owners to specifically address their unique ownership and management situations.

Professional Organizations

Traditionally, most professional service organizations that form a business together have previously been formed as professional corporations or partnerships. These include professional associations of lawyers, accountants, and physicians. However, because the LLC provides limited liability protection for its members, many professionals are now choosing to use this business structure when forming a professional service organization. Professionals are discovering that limited liability companies mitigate most of the shortcomings of the corporation and the partnership. These LLC advantages shield the professional from potentially devastating malpractice awards, double taxation, and involvement — financial or otherwise — in another partner's actions.

Non-Resident and Foreign Business Use

Most nations offered a form of limited liability company for an extensive period before the United States began to sanction the structure. Therefore, foreign businesspeople and investors are familiar with the LLC and its benefits. LLCs also offer the pass-through tax benefits of a partnership with full limited liability protection and no cumbersome citizenship requirements.

Venture Capital Investment

Raising venture capital is a risky undertaking with more traditional business structures. With the limited liability company, on the other hand, a venture capitalist can exercise the desired control, define those situations triggering sale rights, and structure pass-through benefits in the most advantageous manner. At the same time, the venture capitalist can maintain limited liability protection.

Limited Liability Companies:
The Eleven Most Frequently Asked Questions

1. *What is the advantage of an LLC over a general corporation?*

One of the primary reasons individuals form corporations is to protect their personal assets in case of a legal judgment against the company. Unfortunately, owners are taxed twice on their income: once at the corporate level and again at the personal level when dividends are paid.

The LLC, on the other hand, offers both personal asset protection and the elimination of corporate-level taxes. In addition, the recordkeeping requirements of a corporation are far greater than those of the limited liability company.

2. *What is the advantage of the LLC over an S corporation?*

While the S corporation's special tax status eliminates double taxation, it lacks the flexibility of an LLC in allocating income to the owners.

For example, the owner of 25% of an S corporation normally pays 25% of the taxes on reported income. On the other hand, LLC owners are free to divide income and tax liability among themselves within the constraints of IRS regulations for distribution of partnership income. Equal partners may change the allocations of profit or loss from year to year to benefit their individual tax needs.

In addition, LLCs have no ownership restrictions. An S corporation limits the number of owners to just 75 and prohibits corporate and foreign ownership.

3. *Why is the LLC superior to a joint venture or general partnership?*

The personal assets of owners of joint ventures and other forms of general partnerships are totally exposed to lawsuits stemming from the actions of any one partner.

All personal assets of the LLC partners are legally protected. Partnerships of every form and LLCs enjoy a great deal of flexibility compared to corporations when allocating their tax attributes.

4. Why is the LLC superior to a limited partnership?

Limited partners are protected from business-related lawsuits that may place their personal assets at risk. However, this structure prevents them from actively participating in the management of the business. The non-limited partners' personal assets are exposed.

LLCs are designed to protect all partners' personal assets while imposing no limit on their management activity.

5. Why are foreign entrepreneurs attracted to LLCs versus other business structures?

Business entities similar to the limited liability company have been popular in European and Latin American countries for over 100 years. LLCs often prove to be the most familiar and least imposing business structure for foreign entrepreneurs who wish to enter the American market.

There is another clear attraction for foreign owners. If their LLC does not earn income within the U.S., and receives no income from U.S. business enterprises, these foreign owners are normally not subject to U.S. federal income tax.

6. How do I form a limited liability company?

You can form a limited liability company yourself by reading this book and obtaining the necessary forms from the secretary of state of the state in which you want to form the LLC. You may also choose to employ the services of an attorney or a professional service company to aid you.

Professional service companies are low-cost alternatives that completely eliminate all the uncertainty and paperwork involved. One of the nation's largest service companies is:

    Corporate Agents, Inc. (CAI)
    P.O. Box 1281
    1013 Centre Road
    Wilmington, Delaware 19899
    (800) 877-4224

In addition to helping LLC startups for just $99, not including state fees and taxes, CAI can assist in the formation of LLCs or corporations in most foreign jurisdictions.

7. What is the extent of LLC recordkeeping and paperwork?

The limited liability company is usually only required to keep a copy of the Operating Agreement and a list of the LLC members. In most states, owners are not required to make their Operating Agreements public, and they can modify the agreement as needed.

8. Are there special restrictions for selecting an LLC name?

In most states, the name you choose must contain one of the following words: "Company," "Association," "Club," "Foundation," "Fund," "Institute," "Society," "Union," "Syndicate," "Limited," or "Trust." Abbreviations are permitted. In most cases, the name should contain the words "Limited Liability Company" or the abbreviation "L.L.C." Contact your state of formation for specific requirements.

9. Can I convert my corporation into an LLC?

In most states, you can convert your existing corporation to a limited liability company through a merger process. After the new LLC is formed, the merger documents are filed with the secretary of state's office. When filing the merger, the original corporation is listed as the non-surviving entity. After this is completed, you may wish to consult with an attorney or an accountant in order to arrange the most advantageous transfer of the assets to the LLC.

10. How much does it cost to form and maintain an LLC?

To form a limited liability company, you normally only pay the required state filing fees discussed in Chapter 4. Your attorney may add an additional charge on top of the state fees.

A possible middle ground is to use a professional service organization which markets its services to the general public, such as Corporate Agents, Inc.

11. *What are my annual costs for maintaining an LLC?*

Most states levy an annual franchise tax, which ranges from as low as $100 in Delaware to as high as $800 in California. In addition, some states charge an annual filing fee.

Chapter 2

Forming a Limited Liability Company

You should be ready to form your new limited liability company after you review this book and, if you choose, consult a lawyer or an accountant. The regulations and procedures may vary from state to state in their specific details but the essential principals are the same.

There are 10 steps to limited liability company formation that must be followed. These are outlined below.

Step 1: Choosing the State in which to Form the LLC

It is of little advantage to form a limited liability company in a state in which you do not transact business. If you form a limited liability company in Delaware but operate your business in Florida, you will end up paying more. The cost to form a Delaware limited liability company with the help of a service organization would be approximately $250. Florida would consider the Delaware LLC a foreign corporation and require that it pay over $300 in order to qualify to do business in Florida. This would make the total cost $550 rather than only about $250 for forming a Florida LLC in the first place.

You gain the biggest advantage when you form your limited liability company in the state in which you intend to do business.

Step 2: Selecting a Limited Liability Company Name

The second order of business is deciding upon a name. This name must not be in use by another company in the state. Also, it cannot be so similar to another company name that it may cause confusion or mislead the general public in any way.

A name search with the secretary of state or its equivalent division will determine if the proposed name is available. For a small fee, most states will hold a name reservation for up to 120 days to allow time to file for incorporation.

The words "Limited Liability Company" or "Limited Company" or the abbreviations "L.L.C." or "L.C." must follow the selected name. Refer to Chapter 4 for each state's specific requirements on this issue.

Many entrepreneurs use their family name or initials when choosing a company name. However, this choice may cause problems or early setbacks. For example, titles such as Smith, L.L.C. and C.B.A., L.L.C. would probably not pass because it is very likely that companies have already been formed with the same or very similar names.

If you add descriptive words, there is generally a greater chance of acceptance. For example, Smith's Famous Pizza, L.L.C. would most likely be accepted over Smith, L.L.C.

Certain words such as "Bank," "Trust," "Doctor," and "Mortgage" should be avoided because they usually require special approval. In general, the approval process is lengthy and there is a high probability of rejection on the first try.

Step 3: Determining the LLC Address

The LLC address may be a home address or a post office box. Many entrepreneurs use the services of companies that rent private post office boxes to ensure privacy and to keep their personal and business correspondence separate.

Generally, it makes good business sense to choose the address that will be the most convenient to use.

Step 4: Deciding on the Members

Members are the individual(s) who own the company and who set policy. The number of members required varies from state to state, with some states permitting only one member. However, in order to receive federal partnership pass-through tax treatment, the LLC should have at least two members at all times.

Be prepared to provide members' names, addresses, terms of initial appointment, and capital contributions in your Operating Agreement and to state regulating authorities.

Step 5: Declaring the Type of LLC

Many states allow LLC members to choose whether they want to be structured as a corporation or a partnership for tax purposes. If you choose the partnership structure, you will be able to be eligible to benefit from the pass-through tax status.

Step 6: Designating the Organizer

Each state requires someone to file the documents necessary for the organization and formation of the limited liability company. In most states only one person, called the organizer, is necessary to perform this function.

Filing can be accomplished by an attorney, someone close to the limited liability company such as a member or manager, or an employee of a service company who specializes in this type of work.

Step 7: Preparing the Articles of Organization

In order to form a limited liability company in any state, a document called the Articles of Organization, sometimes referred to as a Certificate of Formation, must be written and filed. Many states have simple forms that take very little time to complete. Samples are provided at the end of this chapter for reference use only.

Although specific formation requirements vary from state to state, the Articles of Organization should always be a clear, concise charter of the limited liability company. Minimally, the document normally contains the limited liability company's name and address, the registered agent's name and address within the state, — often called the "registered office" — the members' and managers' names and addresses, and any limiting provisions. See Chapter 4 for the specific requirements for each state.

It is no longer necessary for your LLC to be organized in such a way that the IRS would not consider it a corporation for tax purposes. On January 1, 1997, the Simplification of Entity Classification Rules, 26 CFR Parts 1, 301 and 602 became effective, and eliminated the need to avoid corporate characteristics with the limited liability company.

Your limited liability company must also exhibit certain characteristics described in Chapter 3. These characteristics must be clearly documented in your Articles of Organization in order to eliminate potential IRS problems.

Once the Articles of Organization has been prepared, the organizer(s) files it with the secretary of state. All necessary filing fees must be paid at this time.

If the company name was correctly reserved and the Articles of Organization properly filled out, you should be notified soon afterward that your limited liability company has been accepted by the state and is ready to do business. Do not order supplies or stationery until you have been formally notified that your limited liability company filing has been approved. If you are notified that something is wrong with your filing — for example, the name is already being used or is not allowed — simply correct the problem and refile.

Step 8: Conducting an Organizational Meeting

The first meeting of the company members, called the organizational meeting, should be held as soon as possible after the secretary of state approves the Articles of Organization. At this time, company members determine the Operating Agreement, elect managers and, if necessary, address any business that needs immediate attention.

Step 9: Drafting an Operating Agreement

Most state LLC legislations have rules prescribing how limited liability companies should be operated. Therefore, individuals should obtain a copy of their state's LLC legislation before forming an LLC in order to determine what can and cannot be included in the Operating Agreement.

The Operating Agreement established at the organizational meeting should:

- Approve the Articles of Organization.

- Determine the number of members, method of elections, and grounds for termination.

- Establish the method of choosing managers and their terms, duties, and salaries.

- Clarify times and places for members' meetings, as well as provisions for calling meetings.

- Finalize the principal business address.

- Establish banking procedures and accounts.

- Review procedures for capital contributions and transfers, as well as recordkeeping.

- Outline the authority to change the Operating Agreement as necessary.

Step 10: Applying for Taxpayer Identification

Once you have formed your LLC, it is time to apply for a taxpayer identification number. This is done by completing *Form SS-4*, the employer tax identification number application which can be obtained directly from the IRS. Complete this form and mail it to the same IRS center that will receive the company's federal income tax returns.

You can also obtain your identification number quickly over the telephone by calling (800) 829-1040. Be sure to have your completed *Form SS-4* in front of you when you place this call.

Step 11 (optional): Ordering the LLC Kit

Once the limited liability company has been approved, the organizational meeting has been held, and the Operating Agreement has been finalized, the company is almost ready to conduct business.

At this point, the members may order or buy a limited liability kit. These are available through CAI, Inc., or from stationery stores, business supply outlets, or professional business organizations. These kits include the following items:

Limited Liability Company Seal

The LLC seal is a small hand-held press into which a document is placed to be embossed. The imprint made by the seal includes the company name, state of formation, and the founding date. These seals were once mandatory for corporations, but are now optional in some states.

This seal lends an air of authority to limited liability company documents and is worth having even if the particular state of your LLC does not require it.

Membership Certificate

A membership certificate is a printed certificate used as evidence to show who owns how much of the limited liability company. Most LLC kits contain 10 to 20 blank membership certificates which may be issued as the company sees fit.

Membership certificates are normally accompanied by a membership register which lists the certificates and their current owner(s).

Sample Operating Agreement

To help guide first-time limited liability company owners, most LLC kits contain a sample Operating Agreement to use as a guide or reference on how and why to keep proper records.

For example, meeting minutes are written records of member or other important meetings that must be recorded and documented to prove that the business entity is behaving like a true corporation. Without proper LLC records, a creditor may claim that a company is not a proper LLC and therefore is not entitled to personal asset liability protection.

The Critical Role of the Registered Agent

In most states, a designated person or entity residing in the state of incorporation, known as a registered agent, must be responsible for receiving important legal and tax documents. This service is provided by an agent of the LLC who is registered with the particular state of organization. Registered agents usually perform the following services:

Formation Services

Professional service company registered agents, such as Corporate Agents, Inc., or other types of agents can complete most of the LLC organizational steps outlined in this chapter. In addition, they usually prepare *Form SS-4*, the employer tax identification number application.

Ongoing Services

On a continuing basis, registered agents receive legal and tax documents on behalf of the limited liability company, forward franchise tax and annual report forms to the proper officer(s) of the company, and generally represent the company's interest. In addition, the registered agent may locate a facility for a LLC member meeting or refer a local bank, accountant, or lawyer.

Qualifying Your LLC to Do Business in Other States

When a LLC does business in a state other than its formation state, it is considered a foreign LLC operating in that state.

Owners of foreign, or out-of-state, LLCs should be aware of the potential liabilities, penalties, and problems of operating in another state without properly qualifying in it. Failure to have permission from the proper agencies in the state you plan to do business in may subject your LLC to fines. It may also subject you, and the other members, to criminal charges. In addition, the court system of the state in question may not recognize your LLC's rights in legal matters or contract disputes.

Like the process of forming an LLC, qualifying your LLC to do business in another state is simple to accomplish and can be done without a lawyer.

The 4 Qualifying Steps

To qualify your foreign LLC to do business in another state usually requires these four steps:

1. Obtain documentation from the state of formation indicating your company is a valid LLC in good standing.

2. Complete an application to do business as specified by the secretary of state of the particular state.

3. Designate a registered agent in the state for service of process or other legal documents.

4. Pay the necessary fees and taxes.

Dissolving a Limited Liability Company

This chapter demonstrates how easy it is to form a limited liability company. If you are considering this business structure, it is also important to know that an LLC is just as easy to terminate, or dissolve. Dissolution can occur in two ways:

Involuntary Dissolution

In an involuntary dissolution, the state of formation may terminate a limited liability company for non-payment of the franchise or other taxes it may owe to the state, or for failing to maintain a properly registered agent and registered address within the state.

A judicial dissolution is an involuntary dissolution by a court at the request of the state attorney general, a shareholder, a member, or a creditor.

Voluntary Dissolution

A voluntary dissolution is an action taken by members or directors of a limited liability company to voluntarily dissolve its legal status by using the appropriate statute from the state of formation's LLC legislation.

To dissolve a limited liability company, members normally hold a meeting at which the majority of members vote to terminate the LLC. This action is recorded in the LLC minutes and a resolution is drafted. This resolution authorizes the necessary officers to file a Certificate of Dissolution with the secretary of state.

The appropriate person then calls the secretary of state to determine the particular forms, fees, and procedures required by the limited liability company's state.

Sample Forms to Create Your Own LLC

On the following pages, you will find sample forms to help you start your own limited liability company.

Consult the secretary of state's office in the state in which you plan to operate your limited liability company. Ask if there are any state LLC regulations that must be included in your own paperwork. This state office will also send you the most recent edition of the LLC registration form to complete.

You might also ask the advice of a lawyer or consultant who specializes in this area.

Sample Articles of Organization

Long Version

ARTICLES OF ORGANIZATION For XYZ COMPANY, L.L.C
A LIMITED LIABILITY COMPANY

KNOW ALL MEN BY THESE PRESENTS: That the undersigned desiring to form a limited liability company under the laws of the State of Delaware, do hereby sign, verify and deliver to the Secretary of State of the State of Delaware this Articles of Organization.

ARTICLE I
Name

The name of the limited liability company shall be XYZ Company, L.L.C., a limited liability company (the "Company").

ARTICLE II
Period of Duration

The Company shall exist for a period of thirty (30) years from and after the date the Delaware Secretary of State issues a Certificate of Formation, unless dissolved according to law.

ARTICLE III
Purpose of the Company

The purpose of the Company shall be to engage in any lawful act or activity for which companies may be organized under the Limited Liability Law of Delaware.

ARTICLE IV
Registered Agent and Office

The address of the initial registered office and the principal place of business of the Company is 1013 Centre Road, Wilmington, Delaware

continued on page 25

Sample Articles of Organization *(continued)*

19805, and the name of the registered agent at such address is Corporate Agents, Inc.

ARTICLE V
Contributions

The total amount of cash and the description and agreed value of property contributed to the Company is as follows:

Member	Value of Property	Description
1. J. Doe	$100.00	Cash
2. A. Smith	$100.00	Furniture

ARTICLE VI
Additional Contributions

Unless all members agree in writing, no member shall have any obligation to make any additional contributions to the Company.

ARTICLE VII
Additional Members

The existing members shall have the right to admit additional members to the Company upon such terms and conditions as the existing and additional members shall agree at their sole discretion. Any member who is subsequently admitted as a member of the Company shall have all the rights and obligations of a member under the "Limited Liability Company Agreement."

ARTICLE VIII
Continuation of Business

In the event of the death, retirement, resignation, expulsion, bankruptcy or dissolution of a member or the occurrence of an event which terminates the continued membership of a member in the Company, the remaining members of the Company shall have members,

continued on page 26

Sample Articles of Organization *(continued)*

based on their relative contributions as set forth in ARTICLE V hereof, agree to continue the business of the Company. The remaining members must agree within ninety (90) days from the date of such event whether to continue the business of the Company. In the event the remaining members fail to continue the business of the Company within such ninety (90) day period, the Company shall be dissolved and liquidated.

ARTICLE IX

Manager

The Company shall be managed by one (1) manager. The initial manager of the Company shall be Patrick F. Williams.

The initial manager of the Company shall serve in such capacity pursuant to the Limited Liability Company Agreement until the first meeting of members or until his successor is elected and qualified. At the first annual meeting, and at each annual meeting thereafter, the members shall elect a manager in the manner prescribed by the Limited Liability Company Agreement and he shall serve pursuant to the terms of said Limited Liability Company Agreement.

ARTICLE X

Limited Liability Company Agreement

The regulation of the internal affairs of the Company is more particularly set forth in the Limited Liability Company Agreement.

ARTICLE XI

Transferability of Interests

No interest in the Company may be transferred except as specifically set forth in the Limited Liability Company Agreement.

Dated this _____ day of _____, 199__

_____
J. Doe

_____
A. Smith

Sample Articles of Organization

Short Version

ARTICLES OF INCORPORATION For XYZ COMPANY, L.L.C.
A LIMITED LIABILITY COMPANY

FIRST. The name of this Company shall be XYZ Company, L.L.C., a limited liability company.

SECOND. Its registered office in the State of Delaware is to be located at _____, in the City of _____, County of _____, and its registered agent at such address is _____.

THIRD. The purpose of the Company shall be:

To engage in any lawful act or activity for which a Limited Liability Company may be formed under the Limited Liability Company law of the State of Delaware.

FOURTH. The Company shall exist for a period of thirty (30) years from and after the date the Delaware Secretary of State issues a Certificate of Formation, unless dissolved by law.

FIFTH. The name and mailing address of the persons forming this Limited Liability Company at the instruction of its members is as follows: John Doe, 123 "A" Street, City, State, 45623.

SIXTH. The regulation of the internal affairs of the Company is set forth in the Limited Liability Company Agreement maintained by the members and/or managers.

IN WITNESS WHEREOF, the undersigned, being the individual forming the Company herein before named, as executed, signed and acknowledged this Articles of Organization this _____ day of _____, 199___.

_____

John Doe

Sample LLC Operating Agreement

LIMITED LIABILITY COMPANY OPERATING AGREEMENT
For XYZ COMPANY, L.L.C.

THIS LIMITED LIABILITY COMPANY AGREEMENT (the Agreement) is made and entered into this _____ day of _____, 199___ by:

and each individual or business entity later subsequently admitted to the Company. These individuals and/or business entities shall be known as and referred to as "Members" and individually as a "Member."

_____

_____

As of this date the Members, through their agent, _____, _____ have formed the _____ Limited Liability Company named above under the laws of the State of _____. Accordingly, in consideration of the conditions contained herein, they agree as follows:

ARTICLE I
Company Formation and Registered Agent

1.1 FORMATION. The Members hereby form a Limited Liability Company ("Company") subject to the provisions of the Limited Liability Company Act as currently in effect as of this date. A Certificate of Formation shall be filed with the Secretary of State.

1.2 NAME. The name of the Company shall be:

_____,L.L.C.

1.3 REGISTERED OFFICE AND AGENT. The location of the registered office of the Company shall be

_____

The Company's Registered Agent at such address shall be

_____

continued on page 29

Sample LLC Operating Agreement *(continued)*

1.4 TERM. The Company shall continue for a period of thirty (30) years unless dissolved by:

(a) Members whose capital interest as defined in Article 2.2 exceeds 50 percent vote for dissolution; or

(b) Any event which makes it unlawful for the business of the Company to be carried on by the Members; or

(c) The death, resignation, expulsion, bankruptcy, retirement of a Member or the occurrence of any other event that terminates the continued membership of a Member of the Company; or

(d) Any other event causing a dissolution of a Limited Liability Company under the laws of _____.

1.5 CONTINUANCE OF COMPANY. Notwithstanding the provisions of ARTICLE 1.4, in the event of an occurrence described in ARTICLE 1.4(c), if there are at least two remaining Members, said remaining Members shall have the right to continue the business of the Company. Such right can be exercised only by the unanimous vote of the remaining Members within ninety (90) days after the occurrence of an event described in ARTICLE 1.4(c). If not so exercised, the right of the Members to continue the business of the Company shall expire.

1.6 BUSINESS PURPOSE. The purpose of the Company is to engage in any lawful act or activity for which a Limited Liability Company may be formed under the Limited Liability Law of the State of _____.

1.7 PRINCIPAL PLACE OF BUSINESS. The location of the principal place of business of the Company shall be:

_____

or at such other place as the Managers from time to time select.

1.8 THE MEMBERS. The name and place of residence of each member are contained in Exhibit 2 attached to this Agreement.

continued on page 30

Sample LLC Operating Agreement *(continued)*

ARTICLE 2

Capital Contributions

2.1 INITIAL CONTRIBUTIONS. The Members initially shall contribute to the Company capital as described in Exhibit 3 attached to this Agreement. The agreed value of such property and cash is $_____.

2.2 ADDITIONAL CONTRIBUTIONS. Except as provided in ARTICLE 6.2, no Member shall be obligated to make any additional contribution to the Company's capital.

ARTICLE 3

Profits, Losses and Distributions

3.1 PROFITS/LOSSES. For financial accounting and tax purposes the Company's net profits or net losses shall be determined on an annual basis and shall be allocated to the Members in proportion to each Member's relative capital interest in the Company as set forth in Exhibit 2 as amended from time to time in accordance with Treasury Regulation 1.704-1.

3.2 DISTRIBUTIONS. The Members shall determine and distribute available funds annually or at more frequent intervals as they see fit. Available funds, as referred to herein, shall mean the net cash of the Company available after appropriate provision for expenses and liabilities, as determined by the Managers. Distributions in liquidation of the Company or in liquidation of a Member's interest shall be made in accordance with the positive capital account balances pursuant to Treasury Regulation 1.704-l(b)(2)(ii)(b)(2). To the extent a Member shall have a negative capital account balance, there shall be a qualified income offset, as set forth in Treasury Regulation 1.704-l(b)(2)(ii)(d).

ARTICLE 4

Management

4.1 MANAGEMENT OF THE BUSINESS. The name and place of residence of each Manager is attached as Exhibit 1 of this Agreement.

continued on page 31

Sample LLC Operating Agreement *(continued)*

By a vote of the Members holding a majority of the capital interests in the Company, as set forth in Exhibit 2 as amended from time to time, shall elect so many Managers as the Members determine, but no fewer than one, with one Manager elected by the Members as Chief Executive Manager.

4.2 MEMBERS. The liability of the Members shall be limited as provided under the laws of the Delaware Limited Liability statutes. Members that are not Managers shall take no part whatever in the control, management, direction, or operation of the Company's affairs and shall have no power to bind the Company. The Managers may from time to time seek advice from the Members, but they need not accept such advice, and at all times the Managers shall have the exclusive right to control and manage the Company. No Member shall be an agent of any other Member of the Company solely by reason of being a Member.

4.3 POWERS OF MANAGERS. The Managers are authorized on the Company's behalf to make all decisions as to (a) the sale, development lease or other disposition of the Company's assets; (b) the purchase or other acquisition of other assets of all kinds; (c) the management of all or any part of the Company's assets; (d) the borrowing of money and the granting of security interests in the Company's assets; (e) the prepayment, refinancing or extension of any loan affecting the Company's assets; (f) the compromise or release of any of the Company's claims or debts; and, (g) the employment of persons, firms or corporations for the operation and management of the company's business. In the exercise of their management powers, the Managers are authorized to execute and deliver (a) all contracts, conveyances, assignments leases, subleases, franchise agreements, licensing agreements, management contracts and maintenance contracts covering or affecting the Company's assets; (b) all checks, drafts and other orders for the payment of the Company's funds; (c) all promissory notes, loans, security agreements and other similar documents; and, (d) all other instruments of any other kind relating to the Company's affairs, whether like or unlike the foregoing.

continued on page 32

Sample LLC Operating Agreement *(continued)*

4.4 CHIEF EXECUTIVE MANAGER. The Chief Executive Manager shall have primary responsibility for managing the operations of the Company and for effectuating the decisions of the Managers.

4.5 NOMINEE. Title to the Company's assets shall be held in the Company's name or in the name of any nominee that the Managers may designate. The Managers shall have power to enter into a nominee agreement with any such person, and such agreement may contain provisions indemnifying the nominee, except for his willful misconduct.

4.6 COMPANY INFORMATION. Upon request, the Managers shall supply to any member information regarding the Company or its activities. Each Member or his authorized representative shall have access to and may inspect and copy all books, records and materials in the Manager's possession regarding the Company or its activities. The exercise of the rights contained in this ARTICLE 4.6 shall be at the requesting Member's expense.

4.7 EXCULPATION. Any act or omission of the Managers, the effect of which may cause or result in loss or damage to the Company or the Members if done in good faith to promote the best interests of the Company, shall not subject the Managers to any liability to the Members.

4.8 INDEMNIFICATION. The Company shall indemnify any person who was or is a party defendant or is threatened to be made a party defendant, pending or completed action, suit or proceeding, whether civil, criminal, administrative, or investigative (other than an action by or in the right of the Company) by reason of the fact that he is or was a Member of the Company, Manager, employee or agent of the Company, or is or was serving at the request of the Company, against expenses (including attorney's fees), judgments, fines, and amounts paid in settlement actually and reasonably incurred in connection with such action, suit or proceeding if the Members determine that he acted in good faith and in a manner he reasonably believed to be in or not opposed to the best interest of the Company, and with respect to any criminal action proceeding, has no reasonable cause to believe his/her conduct was unlawful.

The termination of any action, suit, or proceeding by judgment, order, settlement, conviction, or upon a plea of "no lo Contendere" or its

continued on page 33

Sample LLC Operating Agreement *(continued)*

equivalent, shall not in itself create a presumption that the person did or did not act in good faith and in a manner which he reasonably believed to be in the best interest of the Company, and, with respect to any criminal action or proceeding, had reasonable cause to believe that his/her conduct was lawful.

4.9 RECORDS. The Managers shall cause the Company to keep at its principal place of business the following:

(a) a current list in alphabetical order of the full name and the last known street address of each Member;

(b) a copy of the Certificate of Formation and the Company Operating Agreement and all amendments;

(c) copies of the Company's federal, state and local income tax returns and reports, if any, for the three most recent years;

(d) copies of any financial statements of the limited liability company for the three most recent years.

ARTICLE 5

Compensation

5.1 MANAGEMENT FEE. Any Manager rendering services to the Company shall be entitled to compensation commensurate with the value of such services.

5.2 REIMBURSEMENT. The Company shall reimburse the Managers or Members for all direct out-of-pocket expenses incurred by them in managing the Company.

ARTICLE 6

Bookkeeping

6.1 BOOKS. The Managers shall maintain complete and accurate books of account of the Company's affairs at the Company's principal place of business. Such books shall be kept on such method of accounting as the Managers shall select. The company's accounting period shall be the calendar year.

continued on page 34

Sample LLC Operating Agreement *(continued)*

6.2 MEMBER'S ACCOUNTS. The Managers shall maintain separate capital and distribution accounts for each member. Each member's capital account shall be determined and maintained in the manner set forth in Treasury Regulation 1.704-l(b)(2)(iv) and shall consist of his initial capital contribution increased by:

(a) any additional capital contribution made by him/her;

(b) credit balances transferred from his distribution account to his capital account;

and decreased by:

(a) distributions to him/her in reduction of Company capital;

(b) the Member's share of Company losses if charged to his/her capital account.

6.3 REPORTS. The Managers shall close the books of account after the close of each calendar year, and shall prepare and send to each member a statement of such Member's distributive share of income and expense for income tax reporting purposes.

ARTICLE 7

Transfers

7.1 ASSIGNMENT. If at any time a Member proposes to sell, assign or otherwise dispose of all or any part of his interest in the Company, such Member shall first make a written offer to sell such interest to the other Members at a price determined by mutual agreement. If such other Members decline or fail to elect such interest within thirty (30) days, and if the sale or assignment is made and the Members fail to approve this sale or assignment unanimously then, pursuant to Section 18-704(a) of the _____ Limited Liability Company Act, the purchaser or assignee shall have no right to participate in the management of the business and affairs of the Company. The purchaser or assignee shall only be entitled to receive the share of the profits or other compensation by way of income and the return of contributions to which that Member would otherwise be entitled. Signed and Agreed this _____ day of _____199__.

Member_____   Member_____

Sample Listing of Managers

LIMITED LIABILITY COMPANY OPERATING AGREEMENT
FOR _____, L.L.C.

LISTING OF MANAGERS

By a majority vote of the Members the following Managers were elected to operate the Company pursuant to ARTICLE 4 of the Agreement:

NAME: ADDRESS:

_____   _____
Chief Executive Manager   _____

                                 _____

_____   _____

                                 _____

                                 _____

The above listed Manager(s) will serve in their capacities until they are removed for any reason by a majority vote of the Members as defined by ARTICLE 4 or upon their voluntary resignation.

Signed and Agreed this _____ day of _____, 199__.

_____
Member

_____
Member

Sample Listing of Members

LIMITED LIABILITY COMPANY OPERATING AGREEMENT
FOR _____, L.L.C.

LISTING OF MEMBERS

As of the _____ day of _____, 199__ the following is a list of Members of the Company:

NAME: ADDRESS:

_____   _____

                                         _____

                                         _____

_____   _____

                                         _____

                                         _____

Authorized by Member(s) to provide Member Listing

as of this _____ day of _____, 199__

_____

Member

_____

Member

Sample Listing of Capital Contributions

LIMITED LIABILITY COMPANY OPERATING AGREEMENT
FOR _____, L.L.C.

CAPITAL CONTRIBUTIONS

Pursuant to ARTICLE 2, the Members' initial contribution to the Company capital is stated to be $_____. The description and each individual portion of this initial contribution is as follows:

_____ $_____

_____ $_____

_____ $_____

_____ $_____

_____ $_____

_____ $_____

_____ $_____

_____ $_____

_____ $_____

SIGNED AND AGREED this _____ day of _____, 199__.

_____

Member

_____

Member

Chapter 3

Taxation of a Limited Liability Company

The limited liability company combines the corporate advantage of limited personal liability with the pass-through tax advantage of partnerships. This combination provides a distinct alternative to general and limited partnerships and corporations. Other attractive qualities of limited liability companies include the lack of limitations on citizenship requirements, stock, number of members, and ownership by other entities.

Two additional characteristics of the limited liability company make it particularly advantageous from a tax perspective. First, LLCs incur no tax penalties upon liquidation. Second, LLCs can avail themselves of the Section 754 Code Elections. The Section 754 Codes allow for the optional adjustment to basis of partnership (LLC) property.

This chapter will compare the tax implications of the LLC with those of other business entities.

Classification of the LLC for Federal Tax Purposes

In order to understand the tax advantages of the LLC, it is important to review the taxation of the other common types of business entities.

General and close corporations are subject to double taxation. They are first taxed on their net income at the corporate tax rate. Later, at the time they declare their dividends, the shareholders must pay personal income tax on the dividend.

The S corporation, on the other hand, is a pass-through corporate entity. Its income is distributed in proportion to the shareholders' interest in the corporation and they pay personal income tax on the distribution. Limited and general partnerships are also pass-through entities. The partners pay taxes on their proportionate share of profits and losses at their maximum personal rate.

The Qualifying Characteristics

In order for LLCs to receive the same pass-through tax advantage as partnerships, they must follow the rules as set down in the following three court cases: 1) *Morrissey v. Commissioner,*[1] 2) *Larson v. Commissioner,*[2] and *United States v. Kintner.*[3]

It is also important to review the characteristics of an LLC in light of Treasury Regulation 301.7701 (a)–(c). The Regulation lists six major characteristics found in a corporation. These characteristics are:

1. Associates — one or more persons who will participate in the business

2. An objective to carry on business and divide the gains from the business

3. Continuity of life

4. Centralization of management

5. Free transferability of ownership interest

6. Limited liability

In distinguishing the two business entities, the regulation focuses on the last four characteristics because points one and two are essential elements of any business.

A limited liability company is recognized as an unincorporated business and a noncorporate entity — a partnership — as long as no more than two of the last four major corporate characteristics listed above are present.

Therefore, an LLC that exhibits two or fewer of these four corporate characteristics will be characterized as a partnership for tax purposes and have the advantage of pass-through income taxation. The following is a look at each characteristic in detail.

Continuity of Life

The continuity of life characteristic focuses on the effect upon the organization of the termination of membership of one of the members. An entity does not possess continuity of life if the death, mental breakdown, bankruptcy, retirement, resignation, or expulsion of any member will cause a dissolution of the organization.

The Wyoming Limited Liability Act, the first U.S. LLC legislation, states that a limited liability company dissolves following the "death, resignation, expulsion, bankruptcy, and dissolution of a member or of any other events that determines the continuing members of the company." However, under the new tax laws effective January 1, 1997, a LLC is not required to file for dissolution in case of death, expulsion, bankruptcy or insolvency of a member.

A LLC can avoid the continuity of life issue by determining a specified period of time that the LLC may exist. Some states require a predetermined life of 30 years or less spelled out in the Articles of Organization.

Centralization of Management

Centralization of management is present if an individual or group of individuals — often referred to as managers — that does not include all of the company members has continuing exclusive authority over the managerial decisions necessary for the business.

LLCs can avoid this issue by declaring that the business is managed through all the members. However, if managers, who may or may not be the LLC owners, are used to operate the business, it is generally considered to have the characteristic of centralization of management.

Free Transferability of Ownership Interest

Free transferability of ownership interest exists in an entity if any of its invested members can sell or transfer their ownership interest without limitation or be subject to a right of first refusal by the other members.

Limited Liability

The state statutes provide that the limited liability company is entitled to limited liability for all of its members and thus will always have limited liability.

In 1988 the IRS Revenue Ruling 88-76, 1988-2 C.B.360 ruled on the tax treatment of the Wyoming Limited Liability Company Act. The conclusion of the Revenue Ruling stated that the limited liability company under the Wyoming Limited Liability Company Act is classified as a partnership for federal tax purposes.

On October 30, 1994 the IRS released the text of proposed regulation PS 34-92 concerning application of a tax matters partner regulations and procedures to LLC's. Under the proposed regulation an LLC member managers are treated as general partners and nonmanaging members as partners other than general partners. If there are no specified member managers designated by the LLC Articles of Organization then all LLC members will be deemed the equivalent of general partners.

In 1995 the IRS announced a change in policy in IRS Notice 95-14. This Notice proposed rules to allow unincorporated associations like limited liability companies and partnerships to simply make an affirmative election to be taxed as either a partnership or corporation for federal tax purposes. Thus all domestic LLC's with at least two (2) members are eligible to make election under Notice 95-14. In order to make an election under IRS Notice 95-14 all the members of the LLC would be required to sign an original election under the Notice.

In the Spring of 1996 the Treasury Department proposed certain regulations with regard to the simplification of entity classification rules, better known as the "check the box regulations." On December 23, 1996 the Internal Revenue Service published its final regulations on the designation of a tax matters member for limited liability companies. The effect of the new regulations essentially made Revenue Procedure 88-76 obsolete.

On January 1, 1997, the Simplification of Entity Classification Rules, 26 CFR Parts 1, 301 and 602 became effective. With the simplification rules there is now no longer a need to avoid corporate characteristics with the limited liability company.

If a limited liability company has satisfied IRS requirements, it can be treated as a partnership for federal tax purposes. As such, the LLC is required to file the same federal tax forms as a partnership and takes advantage of the same benefits. In addition to the pass-through taxation of a partnership, LLCs are also able to take advantage of the tax allocation methods of partnerships. Partnerships and LLCs specify in their Partnership or Operating Agreement how the profits and losses of the company will be allocated among the members. This allows members to customize their allocations and not base them solely upon the percentage of ownership they possess in the company.

Profits and losses from the LLC that are passed through to the members are reported on their individual income tax forms and paid at their individual tax rate.

Classification of the LLC for State Tax Purposes

Each state legislature has its own set of laws and regulations that govern the taxation of domestic and foreign LLCs.

Although most states follow the federal classification rules as set forth above and will treat LLCs as they are treated on the federal level, some states have special tax arrangements for LLCs. For example, both Texas and Florida require that LLCs pay an annual franchise tax that is not applicable to other entities. Chapter 4 details individual state requirements.

Special Tax Considerations

Tax Basis of LLC Members

An LLC member's tax basis, or total net asset value upon which taxes must be paid, is equal to the member's investment plus the tax value of any property he or she has contributed to the LLC. From this amount, the member must deduct his or her share of the liabilities and debt assumed by the LLC. Finally, this amount is increased or decreased by the member's share of the LLC's income or loss.

Tax Allocation

IRS Section 704 governs the tax allocation of a limited liability company's income, gain, loss, deduction, and credit. These items are allocable if the allocation has substantial economic effect, is in accordance with the LLC members' interests, or is deemed to be in accordance with the members' interest.

At-Risk Rules

Loss allocated to an LLC member under Section 704(b) is tax deductible only to the extent that the member is at risk. The at-risk rules apply to all members of the LLC.

An LLC member will only be at risk to the extent of the value of invested cash plus the tax basis of assets contributed to the LLC. This at-risk amount may decrease through income allocation and increase through additional contributions of capital.

Passive Activity Loss Restrictions

The passive loss restrictions, or passive activity loss restrictions, of IRS Section 469 prevent LLC members from deducting passive activity losses to the extent that the losses exceed the members' income from passive activities. A passive activity is any trade or business in which the taxpayer does not materially participate; this includes any rental activities.

The passive loss limitation rule allows passive activity losses to be carried forward to subsequent years until the member has passive income to offset the losses.

Tax Matters Partner

An LLC manager may be appointed as the tax matters partner (TMP) as long as the LLC manager is an LLC member.

Accounting Method and Taxable Year

If the members actively participate in the limited liability company, the cash method of accounting is available to the LLC.

An LLC that is classified as a tax shelter must use the accrual method. The limited liability company usually selects the calendar year which is consistent with the members' tax reporting calendar.

Tax Advantages of LLCs vs. Other Business Entities

Limited liability companies have several tax advantages as compared to other business entities. These are outlined below.

LLC Advantages Compared to General and Close Corporations

- No corporate-level tax, no double taxation, is assessed.

- No double tax is levied upon liquidation of the company.

- LLCs have the ability to specially allocate profits and losses for pass-through taxation.

- Debt in excess of basis may be contributed to an LLC and avoid gain recognition.

- Liquidating distribution of appreciated property from LLC is not subject to gain.

- Contribution of appreciated assets is not subject to tax.

LLC Advantages Compared to S Corporations

- LLCs can have more than 75 members.

- Tax allocation for LLCs need not be based upon percentage of ownership.

- Non-resident aliens, corporations, partnerships, and trusts can all be members of an LLC.

- LLCs permit more than one class of stock.

- There is a step-up in basis at the death of member under IRS Section 754.

LLC Advantages Compared to Limited Partnerships

- All members are permitted to participate in the management and control of the LLC — unlike limited partners.

- All members have limited personal liability — unlike operating partners.

- Members are not classified as limited partners under the passive loss rules.

Tax Feature Comparison

LLCs vs. Corporations and Partnerships

	LLC	General Corp.	S Corp.	Limited Partnership	General Partnership
Can reduce FICA tax by renting property from owners	Yes	Yes	Yes	Maybe	Maybe
Can easily select fiscal year end	Yes	Yes	No	Maybe	Maybe
Can deduct 100% of owner's health insurance	Yes	Yes	Yes	No	No
Can split income among family members	Yes	Maybe	Yes	Yes	Yes
Can transfer assets "tax free" where debt is less than basis	Yes	No	No	Yes	Yes
Double tax: a. Liquidation b. Earnings c. IRS audit department	No No No	Yes Yes Yes	Maybe No No	No No No	No No No
Able to use lower corporation tax rate	Yes	Yes	No	No	No
Can avoid FICA taxes by: a. Distributions b. Paying children under 18	Yes Yes	No No	Maybe Maybe	No No	No No
Can transfer assets "tax free" where 80% control test is not satisfied	Yes	No	No	Yes	Yes

Tax Feature Comparison

LLCs vs. Corporations and Partnerships

	LLC	General Corp.	S Corp.	Limited Partnership	General Partnership
Can compensate employee with equity	Yes	Yes	Yes	Yes	Yes
Can increase tax basis step-up	Yes	No	No	Yes	Yes
Can use cash method (vs. accrual) even if sales are greater than $5,000,000	Yes	No	Yes	Yes	Yes
Can specially allocate income & expense items	Yes	No	No	Yes	Yes
Can deduct interest paid on money borrowed for investment purposes as business interest	Yes	No	Yes	Yes	Yes
Not subject to a. Alternative Minimum Tax	Yes	No	Yes	Yes	Yes
b. Personal Holding Company	Yes	No	Yes	Yes	Yes
c. Accumulated Earnings Tax	Yes	No	Yes	Yes	Yes
Loss basis includes owner's share of company debt	Yes	No	No	Yes	Yes
Can deduct business loss on individual return & expenses paid personally in figuring AGI	Yes	No	Yes	Yes	Yes

LLC Tax Disadvantages

LLCs have various tax disadvantages as illustrated below. These should be taken into account when considering the LLC relative to other business structures.

- LLCs currently have an individual marginal tax rate of 36.9%, whereas general and close corporations only pay 34%.

- It is not advisable to accumulate large amounts of working capital in an LLC.

- Most states don't allow one-member LLCs, whereas S corporations may have only one shareholder.

- In regards to the passive loss restrictions, there is more certainty about what constitutes material participation by an S corporation shareholder than by an LLC member.

Foreign Inbound Investment

Prior to the 1988 IRS Revenue Ruling which allowed limited liability companies to pass through their taxes, foreign inbound investment into the United States had been utilized typically by general and close corporations and by various partnership entities. Unfortunately, these entities have many tax disadvantages. A review of them is critical to see the major tax advantage of the LLC for foreign inbound investment.

General and Close Corporations

Traditionally, general and close corporations have been used by non-resident aliens to invest in the United States. They typically employ three structures.

1. The non-resident alien may hold 100% of the outstanding shares of stock in a foreign company. The foreign company purchases U.S. real estate or other investments directly from the seller. Thus, the foreign company owns the U.S. real estate or investment.

2. The non-resident alien may establish a two-tier corporate structure to hold the real estate or other investment. First, the non-resident alien forms a foreign company and holds 100% of its outstanding

shares. Second, the foreign company forms a subsidiary in the United States and holds 100% of the outstanding shares of the U.S. subsidiary. Third, the U.S. subsidiary purchases U.S. real estate or other investments.

3. The non-resident alien forms a limited liability company in a foreign jurisdiction to function as a holding company. The foreign jurisdiction holding company forms one or more corporations and maintains ownership of all their shares. Then each of the corporations acquires a single parcel of U.S. real estate.

From a tax perspective, the problem with these alternatives is that the foreign investor must either pay the corporate tax or withhold tax on dividend or royalty income to the foreign parent or foreign shareholders.

S Corporations

A non-resident alien may not invest in the United States through an S corporation due to the IRS restriction that bans non-resident aliens from being shareholders in S corporations.

Partnerships

A non-resident alien may form a general or limited partnership in the United States and be one of its partners. The partnership would then direct the purchase of U.S. real estate or participate in U.S. business activities. If the partnership engages in trade or business in the United States, then the foreign partner would also be treated as engaged in a trade or business.

The taxation of operating profits pass through the partnership to all of the partners. This includes the foreign partner, who is then taxed at the non-resident alien income tax rates.

Limited Liability Companies

Since Revenue Ruling 88-76 states that limited liability company income passes through to its shareholders, LLC shareholders pay tax at their personal rate if they are citizens of the United States.

However, if the shareholder of the LLC is, for example, a foreign corporation located in a tax-haven jurisdiction and owned by a non-resident alien, then its income from the LLC will pass through to the foreign corporation with a withholding tax rate of 30%. This tax rate can be reduced to 5 to 15% through the use of a double tax treaty. This treaty is a reciprocal agreement between two nations that allows the taxpayer to avoid taxation on income by both nations.

Because LLCs are taxed as partnerships, the distribution of earnings to foreign members is taxed at a flat rate of 30% — which can be reduced by treaty — as stipulated by Internal Revenue Code Section 1446. This code states that the partnership (LLC) is required to withhold tax at 30%.

Footnotes

1. *Morrissey v. Commissioner*, 96 U.S. 344 (1935).

2. *Larson v. Commissioner*, 66 T.C. 159 (1976).

3. *United States v. Kintner*, 216 F2d. 418 (9 Cir. 1954).

Chapter 4

Limited Liability Legislation by State

All 50 states plus the District of Columbia recognize limited liability companies as legitimate forms of business. Hawaii and Vermont — the last two states to adopt LLC legislation — now recognize this business entity.

The following listing by state includes the information that is current for each jurisdiction. Be aware, however, that there are frequent changes to telephone numbers, regulations, fees, and other requirements. Check with the referenced source for up-to-date information for your state before proceeding with filing your Articles of Organization.

Alabama

Alabama's limited liability company legislation became effective on October 1, 1993. It recognizes domestic and foreign LLCs.

General Information

Address all correspondence and documentation to:

Alabama Secretary of State
624 State Office Building
Montgomery, AL 36130
(334) 242-5974

Hours: Monday through Friday, 8:00 A.M. to 5:00 P.M.

Fees:

- $5 per name reservation for 120 days.

- $40 LLC formation fee.

- $45 to file Articles of Organization with Judge of Probate.

General Formation Guidelines

1. The name of an Alabama limited liability company must include the term "Limited Liability Company" or the abbreviation "L.L.C." The name must not cause confusion with any other name on file with the secretary of state whether it be that of a corporation, limited partnership, or limited liability company.

2. Two or more people are required to form an Alabama LLC.

3. An original and two copies of the Articles of Organization must be filed with the Judge of Probate in the county of the registered office. Within 10 days of the Judge of Probate's approval, a certified copy of the Articles of Organization must be filed with the secretary of state.

4. The Articles of Organization must include the following eight items:

   - Name of the limited liability company.

   - Purpose for which the LLC was formed.

   - Name and address of the registered agent in Alabama.

   - Period of duration if not perpetual.

   - List of the names and addresses of the initial members.

   - Terms and conditions for admitting new members.

   - Terms and conditions for continuing business after the termination of a member.

   - Statement indicating whether or not the LLC will employ managers to operate the company.

5. Required recordkeeping:

   ▪ List of the names and addresses of all members and managers.

   ▪ Copy of the Articles of Organization and all amendments.

   ▪ Copies of federal, state, and local income tax returns and financial statements for the past three years.

   ▪ Copy of the most current operating agreement.

Alaska

Alaska's limited liability company legislation became effective on July 1, 1995. It recognizes domestic and foreign LLCs.

General Information

Address all correspondence and documentation to:

> Department of Commerce and Economic Development
> Corporations Section
> P.O. Box 110808
> Juneau, AL 99811
> (907) 465-2530

Hours: Monday through Friday, 8:00 A.M. to 5:00 P.M.

Fees:

▪ $250 LLC formation fee (includes first two-year biennial fee).

▪ $100 biennial report and fee due on or before January 2.

General Formation Guidelines

1. The name of an Alaskan LLC must include the term "Limited Liability Company" or the abbreviations "LLC" or "L.L.C." The words "Limited" and "Company" may be abbreviated "Ltd." and "Co.", respectively. The name must not cause confusion with any other name on file with the Department of Commerce and Economic Development whether it be that of a corporation, limited partnership, or limited liability company.

2. Two or more people are required to form an Alaska LLC.

3. An original of the Articles of Organization must be filed with the Department of Commerce and Economic Development.

4. The Articles of Organization must include the following five items:

   ■ Name of the limited liability company.

   ■ Purpose for which the LLC was formed.

   ■ Name and address of the registered agent in Alaska.

   ■ Period of duration if not perpetual.

   ■ Statement indicating whether or not the LLC will employ managers to operate the company.

5. Required recordkeeping:

   ■ List of the names and addresses of all members and managers.

   ■ Copy of the Articles of Organization and all amendments.

   ■ Copies of federal, state, and local income tax returns and financial statements for the past three years.

   ■ Copy of the operating agreement and all amendments.

Arizona

Arizona's limited liability company legislation became effective on September 30, 1993, and was amended in 1994. It recognizes domestic and foreign LLCs.

General Information

Address all correspondence and documentation to:

> Corporations Division
> Arizona Corporation Commission
> 1300 West Washington Street
> Phoenix, AZ 85007
> (602) 542-3135

Hours: Monday through Friday, 8:00 A.M. to 5:00 P.M.

Fees:

- $10 per name reservation.

- $50 LLC formation fee.

- $150 required publishing fee.

- No annual reporting fee.

General Formation Guidelines

1. The name of an Arizona limited liability company must include the terms "Limited Liability Company" or the abbreviations "L.L.C." or "L.C." The name must not cause confusion with any other name on file with the Corporations Division whether it be that of a corporation, limited partnership, or limited liability company.

2. Two or more people are required to form an Arizona LLC.

3. An original and one copy of the Articles of Organization must be filed with the Corporations Division.

4. The Articles of Organization must include the following six items:

   - Name of the limited liability company.

   - Name and address of the registered agent in Arizona.

   - Period of duration if not perpetual.

   - List of the names and addresses of the members and managers.

   - Statement that there are two or more members.

   - Statement indicating whether or not the LLC will employ managers to operate the company.

5. Required recordkeeping:

   - List of the names and addresses of all members and managers.

   - Copy of the Articles of Organization and all amendments.

■ Copies of federal, state, and local income tax returns and financial statements for the past three years.

■ Copy of the operating agreement and all amendments.

Arkansas

Arkansas' limited liability company legislation became effective on April 12, 1993. It recognizes domestic and foreign LLCs.

General Information

Address all correspondence and documentation to:

Corporations Division
Secretary of State of Arkansas
State Capitol
Little Rock, Arkansas 72201
(501) 682-5151

Hours: Monday through Friday, 8:00 A.M. to 4:30 P.M.

Fees:

■ $25 per name reservation.

■ $50 LLC formation fee.

■ $109 annual reporting fee due on or before June 1.

General Formation Guidelines

1. The name of an Arkansas limited liability company must include the terms "Limited Liability Company" or "Limited Company" or the abbreviations "LLC", "LC", "L.L.C.", or "L.C." The words "Limited" and "Company" may be abbreviated "Ltd." and "Co." respectively. The name must not cause confusion with any other name on file with the secretary of state whether it be that of a corporation, limited partnership, or limited liability company.

2. Arkansas allows one person to form an LLC. Be aware that there is no certainty as to how the IRS will classify a one-member LLC.

3. An original and one copy of the Articles of Organization must be filed with the Corporations Division.

4. The Articles of Organization must include the following four items:

   ■ Name of the limited liability company.

   ■ Name and address of the registered agent in Arkansas.

   ■ Period of duration if not perpetual.

   ■ Statement indicating whether or not the LLC will employ managers to operate the company.

5. Required recordkeeping:

   ■ List of the names and addresses of all members and managers.

   ■ Copy of the Articles of Organization and all amendments.

   ■ Copies of federal, state, and local income tax returns and financial statements for the past three years.

   ■ Copy of the operating agreement and all amendments.

California

California's limited liability company legislation became effective on September 30, 1994. It recognizes domestic and foreign LLCs.

General Information

Address all correspondence and documentation to:

> Secretary of State/Limited Liability Company Unit
> 1500 11th Street, Third Floor
> Sacramento, CA 95814
> (916) 653-3795

Hours: Monday through Friday, 8:00 A.M. to 5:00 P.M.

Fees:

■ $10 per name reservation for 60 days. Can be renewed one time.

■ $70 LLC formation fee.

- $800 franchise tax payable within 3 months of formation if taxed as a partnership.

- $800 franchise tax payable at time of formation if taxed as a corporation.

- $800 annual franchise tax due within 3 months of close of accounting year.

General Formation Guidelines

1. The name of a California limited liability company must include the term "Limited Liability Company" or the abbreviation "L.L.C." The words "Limited" and "Company" may be abbreviated "Ltd." and "Co." respectively. The name must not cause confusion with any other name on file with the secretary of state whether it be that of a corporation, limited partnership, or limited liability company.

2. Two or more people are required to form a California LLC.

3. An original and one copy of the Articles of Organization must be filed with the secretary of state.

4. The Articles of Organization must include the following five items:

   - Name of the limited liability company.

   - The following statement:

   "The purpose of the limited liability company is to engage in any lawful act or activity for which a limited liability company may be organized under the Beverly–Killea Limited Liability Company Act."

   - Name and address of the registered agent in California.

   - Period of duration if not perpetual.

   - Statement indicating whether or not the LLC will employ managers to operate the company.

5. Required recordkeeping:

   - List of the names and last known addresses of members and other holders with an economic interest in the LLC together with their contributions and their shares in profits and losses.

- Copy of the Articles of Organization and all amendments.

- Copies of federal, state, and local income tax returns and financial statements for the past six years.

- Copy of the operating agreement and all amendments.

Colorado

Colorado's limited liability company legislation became effective on April 18, 1990, and was amended in 1994. It recognizes domestic and foreign LLCs.

General Information

Address all correspondence and documentation to:

Division of Commercial Recordings
Secretary of State
1560 Broadway, Suite 200
Denver, CO 80202
(303) 894–2251

Hours: Monday through Friday, 8:00 A.M. through 5:00 P.M.

Fees:

- $10 per name reservation for 120 days.

- $50 LLC formation fee.

- $25 biennial reporting fee.

General Formation Guidelines

1. The name of a Colorado limited liability company must include the term "Limited Liability Company" or the abbreviation "LLC". The name must not cause confusion with any other name on file with the secretary of state whether it be that of a corporation, limited partnership, or limited liability company.

2. Colorado allows one person to form an LLC. Be aware that there is no certainty as to how the IRS will classify a one-member LLC.

3. Two original copies of the Articles of Organization must be filed with the Division of Commercial Recordings.

4. The Articles of Organization must include the following six items:

    ■ Name of the limited liability company.

    ■ Principal office address.

    ■ Name and address of the registered agent in Colorado.

    ■ If members are to operate the company, the names and addresses of the members.

    ■ If managers are to operate the company, the names and business addresses of the managers.

    ■ Statement indicating whether or not the LLC will employ managers to operate the company.

    Colorado does not require a statement indicating the duration of the LLC. However, to avoid federal income tax problems a period of duration should be included in the Articles of Organization.

5. Required recordkeeping:

    ■ List of the names and addresses of all past and present members and managers.

    ■ Certified statement listing each member's cash and other contributions and right of termination if not already included in the operating agreement.

    ■ Copy of the Articles of Organization and all amendments

    ■ Copies of federal and state income tax returns and financial statements for the past three years.

    ■ Copy of the most current operating agreement and all amendments.

    ■ Minutes of every meeting.

Connecticut

Connecticut's limited liability company legislation became effective on October 1, 1993. It recognizes domestic and foreign LLCs.

General Information

Address all correspondence and documentation to:

> Secretary of State
> 30 Trinity Street
> Hartford, CT 06106
> (860) 566-8574
> (860) 566-8570 (Name availability)

Hours: Monday through Friday, 10:00 A.M. to 2:55 P.M. for new filings. Telephone calls are accepted from 8:30 A.M. to 4:25 P.M.

Fees:

- $30 per name reservation for 120 days.

- $60 LLC formation fee.

- $10 annual reporting fee.

General Formation Guidelines

1. The name of a Connecticut limited liability company must include the term "Limited Liability Company" or the abbreviations "LLC" or "L.L.C." The words "Limited" and "Company" may be abbreviated "Ltd." and "Co." respectively. The name must not cause confusion with any other name on file with the secretary of state whether it be that of a corporation, limited partnership, or limited liability company.

2. Two or more people are required to form a Connecticut LLC.

3. Two copies of the Articles of Organization must be filed with the secretary of state.

4. The Articles of Organization must include the following four items:

   - Name of the limited liability company.

   - Purpose for which the LLC was formed.

   - Period of duration if not perpetual.

   - Statement indicating whether or not the LLC will employ managers to operate the company.

5. Required recordkeeping:

   - List of the names and addresses of all past and present members and managers.

   - List of members' cash and other contributions.

   - Copy of the Articles of Organization and all amendments.

   - Copies of federal, state, and local income tax returns and financial statements for the past three years.

   - Copies of written operating agreements no longer in effect.

   - Rights and conditions for terminating the company.

   - Copy of current operating agreement.

Delaware

Delaware's limited liability company legislation became effective on October 1, 1992, and was amended in 1994 and 1995. It recognizes domestic and foreign LLCs.

General Information

Address all correspondence and documentation to:

Corporate Filing Section, Division of Corporations
Secretary of State
John G. Townsend Building
P.O. Box 7040
Dover, DE 19903
(302) 739-3073 — General Information
(900) 420-8042 — Name Reservation

Hours: Monday through Friday, 8:30 A.M. to 4:30 P.M.

Fees:

- $10 per name reservation for 120 days.

- $70 LLC formation fee.

- $100 annual reporting fee due on or before June 1.

General Formation Guidelines

1. The name of a Delaware limited liability company must include the term "Limited Liability Company" or the abbreviation "L.L.C." The name may contain the words "Company", "Association", "Club", "Foundation", "Fund", "Institute", "Society", "Union", "Syndicate", "Limited", "Trust", or their abbreviations. The name may contain the name of a member or manager. The name must not cause confusion with any other name on file with the secretary of state whether it be that of a corporation, limited partnership, or limited liability company.

2. Delaware allows one person to form a limited liability company. However, please be aware that there is no certainty as to how the IRS will classify a one-member LLC.

3. An original copy of the Articles of Organization must be filed with the secretary of state.

4. The Articles of Organization must include the following three items:

    ■ Name of the limited liability company.

    ■ Principal office address.

    ■ Name and address of the registered agent in Delaware.

    Delaware does not require a statement indicating the duration of the LLC. However, to avoid federal income tax problems, a period of duration should be included in the Articles of Organization.

5. Required recordkeeping:

    ■ Delaware imposes no recordkeeping requirements on LLCs and does not require LLCs to distribute regular reports to its members. The LLC should maintain minutes of the meetings of the members and managers of the company, however, and should also keep a copy of the operating agreement.

6. Special advantages of forming a Delaware LLC:

    ■ Historically, Delaware has kept its business formation fees low and is one of the friendliest states to corporations and LLCs. Indeed, nearly 50 % of all the companies listed on the New York Stock Exchange and almost one third of all companies listed on the American Stock Exchange are incorporated in Delaware.

- There is no minimum capital requirement to organize a Delaware corporation or LLC and no need to have a bank account in Delaware.

- One person is permitted to hold all of the offices of the company (e.g., president, vice president, secretary, and treasurer). Many states require several different officers.

- There is no state business income tax on Delaware LLCs which do not earn income within the state.

- Shares of a Delaware LLC owned by persons residing outside of Delaware are not subject to Delaware personal income tax.

- There is no Delaware inheritance tax levied on ownership interest in LLCs held by non-residents.

- Delaware is the only state which maintains a separate court system for business. It is called the Court of Chancery.

District of Columbia

The District of Columbia's limited liability company legislation became effective on July 23, 1994. It recognizes domestic and foreign LLCs.

General Information

Address all correspondence and documentation to:

Department of Consumer Regulatory Affairs
Business Regulation Administration
Room 407
Washington, D.C. 20001
(202) 727-7287

Hours: Monday through Friday, 9:00 A.M. to 2:00 P.M.

Fees:

- $25 per name reservation for 60 days.

- $100 LLC formation fee.

- $50 required annual reporting fee due on or before June 16th of each year.

General Formation Guidelines

1. The name of a D.C. limited liability company must include the term "Limited Liability Company" or the abbreviation "L.L.C." The name must not cause confusion with any other name on file with the Business Regulation Administration whether it be that of a corporation, limited partnership, or limited liability company.

2. Two or more people are required to form a District of Columbia LLC.

3 An original and one copy of the Articles of Organization must be filed with the Department of Consumer Regulatory Affairs.

4. The Articles of Organization must include the following three items:

   - Name of the limited liability company

   - Name and address of the registered agent in D.C. and evidence of the registered agent's consent to serve

   - Period of duration if not perpetual.

5. Required recordkeeping:

   - List of the names and addresses of all members

   - Copy of the Articles of Organization and all amendments

   - Copies of federal, state, and local income tax returns for the past three years

   - Copy of most current operating agreement.

Florida

Florida's LLC legislation became effective on April 21, 1982, and was amended in 1993. It recognizes domestic and foreign LLCs.

General Information

Address all correspondence and documentation to:

Division of Corporations
Department of State
409 East Gaines Street
Tallahassee, FL 32314
(904) 487-6052
(904) 488-9000 (Name availability)

Hours: Monday through Friday, 8:00 A.M. to 4:30 P.M.

Fees:

- $35 per name of registered agent.

General Formation Guidelines

1. The name of a Florida limited liability company must include the terms "Limited Liability Company" or "Limited Company" or the abbreviations "LLC", "L.L.C.", or "L.C." The name must not cause confusion with any other name on file with the Department of State whether it be that of a corporation, limited partnership, or an LLC.

2. Two or more people are required to form a Florida LLC.

3. An original and one copy of the Articles of Organization must be filed with the Division of Corporations.

4. The Articles of Organization must include the following six items:

   - Name of the limited liability company.

   - Principal mailing and street address.

   - Period of duration if not perpetual.

   - Rights, terms, and conditions of admission of new members by current members.

   - Rights and conditions of company continuation upon the termination of a member.

   - Statement indicating whether the LLC will be operated by managers or members together with their names and addresses.

5. Required recordkeeping:

   - List of the names and addresses of all members.

   - List of members' cash and other contributions if not already included in the Articles of Organization.

- Copy of the Articles of Organization and all amendments.

- Copies of federal, state, and local income tax returns and financial statements for the past three years.

Georgia

Georgia's limited liability company legislation became effective on March 1, 1994. It recognizes domestic and foreign LLCs.

General Information

Address all correspondence and documentation to:

Business Services and Regulation
Secretary of State
2 Martin Luther King, Jr. Drive, S.E.
Suite 315, West Tower
Atlanta, GA 30334-1530
(404) 656-2811 (General Information)
(404) 656-2817 (Name Reservation)

Hours: Monday through Friday, 8:00 A.M. to 4:30 P.M.

Fees:

- $75 LLC formation fee.

- $25 required annual reporting fee due between January 1 and April 15.

General Formation Guidelines

1. The name of a Georgia limited liability company must include the terms "Limited Liability Company" or "Limited Company" or the abbreviations "L.L.C.", "L.C.", "LLC", or "LC". The words "Limited" and "Company" may be abbreviated "Ltd." and "Co." respectively. The name must not cause confusion with any other name on file with the secretary of state whether it be that of a corporation, limited partnership, or limited liability company.

2. Georgia allows one person to form an LLC. However, please be aware that there is no certainty as to how the IRS will classify a one-member LLC.

3. An original and one copy of the Articles of Organization must be filed with the Business Services and Regulation department.

4. The Articles of Organization must include the following four items:

    ■ Name of the limited liability company.

    ■ Name and address of the registered agent in Georgia.

    ■ Period of duration if not perpetual.

    ■ Statement indicating whether or not the company will employ managers to operate the company.

5. Required recordkeeping:

    ■ List of the names and addresses of all members and managers.

    ■ Copy of the Articles of Organization and all amendments.

    ■ Copies of federal, state, and local income tax returns and financial statements for the past three years.

    ■ Copies of records that would enable a member to determine the relative voting rights, if any, of the members.

    ■ Copy of the operating agreement and all amendments.

Hawaii

Hawaii adopted limited liability company legislation effective April 1, 1997. It recognizes domestic and foreign LLCs.

General Information

Address all correspondence and documentation to:

> Hawaii Department of Commerce and Consumer Affairs
> 1010 Richards Street
> Honolulu, HI 96813
> (808) 586-2727

Hours: Monday through Friday, 8:00 A.M. to 5:00 P.M.

Fees:

■ $100 domestic LLC formation fee.

■ $100 foreign LLC formation fee.

■ $25 annual reporting fee.

General Formation Guidelines

1. The name of an Hawaii limited liability company must include the terms "Limited Liability Company," or the abbreviation "L.L.C." or "LLC." The name must not cause confusion with any other name on file with the Department of Commerce and Consumer Affairs whether it be that of a corporation, limited partnership, or limited liability company.

2. The Articles of Organization must include the following six items:

   ■ The street address of the company's initial designated office in Hawaii. If no specific street address is available, state the rural route post office number or post office box designated by the U.S. Post Office.

   ■ The name and street address of the company's agent for service of process.

   ■ The name and street address of each organizer of the company.

   ■ Indicate whether the period of duration of the company is at-will or for a specified term. Include the expiration date if the duration is for a specified term.

   ■ State whether the company is manager-managed or member-managed. Include the names and residence street addresses of either the initial managers, if manager-managed, or the initial members if member-managed.

   ■ Indicate whether the members are liable or not liable for the debts, obligations and liability of the company.

3. Two or more people are required to form a Hawaii LLC.

4. Required recordkeeping:

   ■ A list of the names and addresses of all past and present members and managers and the date on which each became a member.

   ■ Copy of the Articles of Organization and all amendments.

   ■ Copies of federal, state, and local income tax returns and financial statements for the past three years.

   ■ Copy of the operating agreement and all amendments.

Idaho

Idaho's limited liability company legislation became effective on July 1, 1993, and was amended in 1994. It recognizes domestic and foreign LLCs.

General Information

Address all correspondence and documentation to:

> Secretary of State
> P.O. Box 83720
> Boise, ID 83720
> (208) 334-2300 Ext. 0080

Hours: Monday through Friday, 8:00 A.M. through 5:00 P.M.

Fees:

- $20 per name reservation for four months.

- $100 LLC formation fee.

- No annual reporting fee.

- Annual report must be filed between July 1 and November 1.

General Formation Guidelines

1. The name of an Idaho limited liability company must include the terms "Limited Liability Company" or "Limited Company" or the abbreviations "L.L.C." or "L.C." The words "Limited" and "Company" may be abbreviated "Ltd." and "Co." respectively. The name must not cause confusion with any other name on file with the secretary of state whether it be that of a corporation, limited partnership, or limited liability company.

2. Idaho allows one person to form an LLC. However, please be aware that there is no certainty as to how the IRS will classify a one-member LLC.

3. An original and one copy of the Articles of Organization must be filed with the secretary of state.

4. The Articles of Organization must include the following four items:

- Name of the limited liability company.

- Name and address of the registered agent in Idaho.

- Period of duration if not perpetual.

- Statement indicating whether or not the LLC will employ managers to operate the company.

5. Required recordkeeping:

    - List of the names and addresses of all past and present members and managers.

    - Copy of the Articles of Organization and all amendments.

    - Copies of federal, state, and local income tax returns and financial statements for the past three years.

    - Copy of the operating agreement and all amendments.

Illinois

Illinois' limited liability company legislation became effective on January 1, 1994. It recognizes domestic and foreign LLCs.

General Information

Address all correspondence and documentation to:

> Department of Business Services
> Illinois Secretary of State
> Limited Liability Company Division
> Room 359, Howlett Building
> Springfield, IL 62756
> (217) 524-8008

Hours: Monday through Friday, 8:00 A.M. to 4:30 P.M.

Fees:

- $300 per name reservation for 90 days.

- $500 LLC formation fee.

- $300 required annual reporting fee.

General Formation Guidelines

1. The name of an Illinois limited liability company must include the term "Limited Liability Company" or the abbreviation "L.L.C." The name must not cause confusion with any other name on file with the Illinois Secretary of State whether it be that of a corporation, limited partnership, or limited liability company.

2. Two or more people are required to form an Illinois LLC.

3. An original and one copy of the Articles of Organization must be filed with the Department of Business Services.

4. The Articles of Organization must include the following seven items:

    - Name of the limited liability company.

    - Purpose for which the LLC was formed.

    - Name and address of the registered agent in Illinois.

    - Period of duration if not perpetual.

    - List of the names and addresses of the managers, if any.

    - List of the names and addresses of the members if the company is not going to employ managers.

    - Names and addresses of each organizer.

5. Required recordkeeping:

    - A list of the names and addresses of all members, each members' cash and other contributions, and the date on which each became a member.

    - Description and statement of the agreed-upon value of the property or services each member has contributed or has agreed to contribute in the future.

    - Copy of the Articles of Organization and all amendments.

    - Copies of federal, state, and local income tax returns and financial statements for the past three years.

    - Copy of the operating agreement and all amendments.

Indiana

Indiana's limited liability company legislation became effective on July 1, 1993, and was amended in 1994. It recognizes domestic and foreign LLCs.

General Information

Address all correspondence and documentation to:

Corporations Division
Indiana Secretary of State
Room E-018
302 West Washington Street
Indianapolis, IN 46204
(317) 232-6576

Hours: Monday through Friday, 8:15 A.M. to 5:30 P.M., and Saturday, 9:00 A.M. to noon.

Fees:

- $20 per name reservation for 120 days.

- $90 LLC formation fee.

- $30 biennial reporting fee.

General Formation Guidelines

1. The name of an Indiana limited liability company must include the term "Limited Liability Company" or the abbreviations "L.L.C." or "LLC". The name must not cause confusion with any other name on file with the secretary of state whether it be that of a corporation, limited partnership, or limited liability company.

2. Two or more people are required to form an Indiana LLC.

3. An original and one copy of the Articles of Organization must be filed with the Corporations Division.

4. The Articles of Organization must include the following four items:

   - Name of the limited liability company.

- Name and address of the registered agent in Indiana.

- Period of duration if not perpetual.

- Statement indicating whether or not the LLC will employ a manager to operate the company.

5. Required recordkeeping:

    - List of the names and addresses of all members and managers.

    - Copy of the Articles of Organization and all amendments.

    - Copies of federal, state, and local income tax returns and financial statements for the past three years.

    - Copy of the operating agreement and all amendments.

Iowa

Iowa's limited liability company legislation became effective on July 1, 1992, and was amended in 1993. It recognizes domestic and foreign LLCs.

General Information

Address all correspondence and documentation to:

> Corporations Department
> Secretary of State
> Second Floor
> Hoover Building
> Des Moines, IA 50319
> (515) 281-5204

Hours: Monday through Friday, 8:00 A.M. to 4:30 P.M.

Fees:

- $10 per name reservation for 120 days.

- $50 LLC formation fee.

- No annual reporting fee required.

General Formation Guidelines

1. The name of an Iowa limited liability company must include the term "Limited Company" or the abbreviation "L.C." The name must not cause confusion with any other name on file with the secretary of state whether it be that of a corporation, limited partnership, or limited liability company.

2. Two or more people are required to form an Iowa LLC.

3. An original and one copy of the Articles of Organization must be filed with the Corporations Department.

4. The Articles of Organization must include the following four items:

    ■ Name of the limited liability company.

    ■ Principal office address.

    ■ Name and address of the registered agent in Iowa.

    ■ Period of duration if not perpetual.

5. Required recordkeeping:

    ■ List of the names and addresses of all members and managers.

    ■ Copy of the Articles of Organization and all amendments.

    ■ Copies of federal, state, and local income tax returns and financial statements for the past three years.

    ■ Copy of the operating agreement and all amendments.

Kansas

Kansas's limited liability company legislation became effective on July 1, 1990, and was amended in 1994. It recognizes domestic and foreign LLCs.

General Information

Address all correspondence and documentation to:

Office of the Secretary of State
300 S.W. 10th; 2nd floor
State Capitol
Topeka, KS 66612
(913) 296-4564

Hours: Monday through Friday, 8:00 A.M. to 5:00 P.M.

Fees:

- $20 per name reservation for 120 days.

- $150 LLC formation fee.

- Minimum $20 annual reporting fee.

General Formation Guidelines

1. The name of an Kansas limited liability company must include the terms "Limited Liability Company" or "Limited Company" or the abbreviations "L.L.C.", "L.C.", "LLC" or "LC." The name must not cause confusion with any other name on file with the secretary of state whether it be that of a corporation, limited partnership, or limited liability company.

2. Two or more people are required to form a Kansas LLC.

3. An original and one copy of the Articles of Organization must be filed with the secretary of state.

4. The Articles of Organization must include the following seven items:

   - Name of the limited liability company.

   - Purpose for which the LLC was formed.

   - Name and address of the registered agent in Kansas.

   - Period of duration if not perpetual.

   - Rights and conditions for admitting new members.

   - Rights and conditions for continuing business after the termination of a member.

   - Statement indicating whether or not the LLC will employ managers to operate the company.

5. Required recordkeeping:

   ■ List of the names and addresses of all members and managers.

   ■ Copy of the Articles of Organization and all amendments.

   ■ Copies of federal, state, and local income tax returns and financial statements for the past three years.

   ■ Detailed minutes of all management meetings including all resolutions involving business matters.

Kentucky

Kentucky's limited liability company legislation became effective on July 15, 1994. It recognizes domestic and foreign LLCs.

General Information

Address all correspondence and documentation to:

> Secretary of State
> P.O. Box 718
> Frankfort, KY 40602-0718
> (502) 564-2848

Hours: Monday through Friday, 8:30 A.M. to 4:30 P.M.

Fees:

■ $15 per name reservation for 120 days.

■ $40 LLC formation fee.

■ $15 required annual reporting fee due between January 1 and June 30.

General Formation Guidelines

1. The name of a Kentucky limited liability company must include the term "Limited Liability Company" or the abbreviations "LLC" or "LC". The name must not cause confusion with any other name on file with the secretary of state whether it be that of a corporation, limited partnership, or limited liability company.

2. Two or more people are required to form a Kentucky LLC.

3. An original and one copy of the Articles of Organization must be filed with the secretary of state.

4. The Articles of Organization must include the following six items:

   - Name of the limited liability company.

   - Mailing address of the principal office.

   - Name and address of the registered agent in Kentucky.

   - Period of duration if not perpetual.

   - Statement that there are at least two or more members.

   - Statement indicating whether or not the LLC will employ managers to operate the company.

5. Required recordkeeping:

   - List of the names and addresses of all members and managers.

   - Copy of the Articles of Organization and all amendments.

   - Copies of federal, state, and local income tax returns for the past three years and financial statements for the past five years.

   - Copy of the operating agreement and all amendments.

Louisiana

Louisiana's limited liability company legislation became effective on July 7, 1992. It recognizes domestic and foreign LLCs.

General Information

Address all correspondence and documentation to:

Secretary of State
Commercial Division
P.O. Box 94125
Baton Rouge, LA 70804
(504) 925-4704

Hours: Monday through Friday, 8:20 A.M. to 4:30 P.M.

Fees:

- $20 per name reservation for 60 days.

- $60 LLC formation fee.

- $25 annual reporting fee.

- $20 county recording fee.

General Formation Guidelines

1. The name of a Louisiana limited liability company must include the term "Limited Liability Company" or the abbreviations "L.L.C." or "L.C." The name must not cause confusion with any other name on file with the secretary of state whether it be that of a corporation, limited partnership, or limited liability company.

2. Two or more people are required to form a Louisiana LLC.

3. An original and one copy of the Articles of Organization must be filed with the secretary of state.

4. The Articles of Organization must include the following three items:

    - Name of the limited liability company.

    - Purpose for which the LLC was formed.

5. Required recordkeeping:

    - List of the names and addresses of all members and managers.

    - Copy of the Articles of Organization and all amendments.

    - Copies of federal, state, and local income tax returns and financial statements for the past three years.

    - Copy of the most current operating agreement and all amendments.

Maine

Maine's limited liability company legislation became effective on January 1, 1995. It recognizes domestic and foreign LLCs.

General Information

Address all correspondence and documentation to:

State Department
Bureau of Corporations
101 State House Station
Augusta, ME 04333
(207) 287-4190

Hours: Monday through Friday, 8:00 A.M. to 5:00 P.M.

Fees:

- $20 per name reservation for 120 days.

- $250 LLC formation fee.

- $60 annual reporting fee.

General Formation Guidelines

1. The name of a Maine limited liability company must include the term "Limited Liability Company." The name must not cause confusion with any other name on file with the secretary of state whether it be that of a corporation, limited partnership, or LLC.

2. Two or more people are required to form a Maine LLC.

3. An original and one copy of the Articles of Organization must be filed with the secretary of state.

4. The Articles of Organization must include the following four items:

   - Name of the limited liability company.

   - Name and address of the registered agent in Maine.

   - Statement indicating whether or not the LLC will employ managers to operate the company and, if so, the number of managers permitted.

   - Names and business, residence, or mailing addresses of all the managers, if the LLC is going to employ managers and if they have been selected.

5. Required recordkeeping:

   - List of the names and addresses of all past and present members and managers.

   - Copy of the Articles of Organization and all amendments.

   - Copy of the operating agreement and all amendments.

Maryland

Maryland's limited liability company legislation became effective on October 1, 1992. It recognizes domestic and foreign LLCs.

General Information

Address all correspondence and documentation to:

Charter Division
Maryland State Department of Assessments and Taxation
Room 809
301 West Preston Street
Baltimore, MD 21201
(410) 225-1330

Hours: Monday through Friday, 8:00 A.M. to 4:30 P.M.

Fees:

- $7 per name reservation for 30 days.

- $50 LLC formation fee.

- $50 reporting fee filed every five years.

General Formation Guidelines

1. The name of a Maryland limited liability company must include the term "Limited Liability Company" or the abbreviations "L.L.C.", "LLC", "L.C." or "LC", The name must not cause confusion with any other name on file with the State Department of Assessments and Taxation whether it be that of a corporation, limited partnership, or limited liability company.

2. Two or more people are required to form a Maryland LLC.

3. An original and one copy of the Articles of Organization must be filed with the Charter Division.

4. The Articles of Organization must include the following five items:

    ■ Name of the limited liability company.

    ■ Principal office address in Maryland.

    ■ Purpose for which the LLC was formed.

    ■ Name and address of the registered agent in Maryland.

    ■ Period of duration if not perpetual.

5. Required recordkeeping:

    ■ Maryland imposes no recordkeeping requirements on LLCs. However, the LLC should keep:

        ■ List of the names and addresses of all members.

        ■ Copy of the Articles of Organization and all amendments.

        ■ Copies of all federal, state, and local income tax returns and financial statements for the past three years.

Massachusetts

Massachusetts' limited liability company legislation became effective on January 1, 1996. It recognizes domestic and foreign LLCs.

General Information

Address all correspondence and documentation to:

> Corporations Division
> Secretary of State
> One Ashburton Place
> Boston, MA 02108
> (617) 727-2850

Hours: Monday through Friday, 8:00 A.M. to 5:00 P.M.

Fees:

- $15 per name reservation.

- $500 LLC formation fee.

- $500 annual reporting fee.

General Formation Guidelines

1. The name of a Massachusetts limited liability company must include the terms "Limited Liability Company" or "Limited Company" or the abbreviations "LC", "L.C.", "L.L.C." or "LLC." The name must not cause confusion with any other name on file with the secretary of state whether it be that of a corporation, limited partnership, or limited liability company.

2. Massachusetts allows one person to form an LLC. Be aware that there is no certainty as to how the IRS will classify a one-member LLC.

3. The address of an office in the commonwealth is required for filing.

4. The Articles of Organization must include the following five items:

   - Name of the limited liability company.

   - Name and address of the registered agent in Massachusetts.

   - A specific date of dissolution.

   - If the LLC has managers at the time of its formation, the name and address of each manager is required.

   - The specific purpose of the LLC.

5. Required recordkeeping:

   - List of the names and addresses of all managers.

   - Copy of the Articles of Organization and all amendments.

Michigan

Michigan's limited liability company legislation became effective on June 1, 1993. It recognizes domestic and foreign LLCs.

General Information

Address all correspondence and documentation to:

> Corporations Division
> Michigan Department of Commerce
> P.O. Box 30054
> Lansing, MI 48909
> (517) 334-6301
> (900) 555-0031 (Name availability)

Hours: Monday through Friday, 8:00 A.M. to 5:00 P.M.

Fees:

- $10 per name reservation for 120 days.

- $50 LLC formation fee.

- $5 reporting fee.

General Formation Guidelines

1. The name of an Michigan limited liability company must include the terms "Limited Liability Company" or the abbreviations "L.L.C." or "L.C." The name must not cause confusion with any other name on file with the Corporations Division whether it be that of a corporation, limited partnership, or limited liability company.

2. Two or more people are required to form an Michigan LLC.

3. An original and one copy of the Articles of Organization must be filed with the Corporations Division.

4. The Articles of Organization must include the following six items:

   - Name of the limited liability company.

   - Purpose for the existence of the LLC.

   - Name and address of the registered agent in Michigan.

   - A period of duration is not required, but a date for dissolution must be set.

- List of the names and addresses of the members.

- Statement indicating whether or not the LLC will employ managers to operate the company.

5. Required recordkeeping:

   - List of the names and addresses of all members and managers.

   - Copy of the Articles of Organization and all amendments.

   - Copies of federal, state, and local income tax returns and financial statements for the past three years.

   - Copy of the operating agreement and all amendments.

   - Any and all records determining ownership distributions of the members and the rights of members to vote in LLC matters.

Minnesota

Minnesota's limited liability company legislation became effective on January 1, 1993. It recognizes domestic and foreign LLCs.

General Information

Address all correspondence and documentation to:

> Secretary of State
> 180 State Office Building
> St. Paul, MN 55155-1299
> (612) 296-2803

Hours: Monday through Friday, 8:00 A.M. to 4:30 P.M.

Fees:

- $35 per name reservation for one year.

- $135 LLC formation fee.

- No annual reporting fee. Biennial report due date based on annual LLC formation.

General Formation Guidelines

1. The name of a Minnesota limited liability company must include the terms "Limited Liability Company" or the abbreviation "L.L.C." The name must not cause confusion with any other name on file with the secretary of state whether it be that of a corporation, limited partnership, or limited liability company.

2. Two or more members are required for a Minnesota LLC.

3. One copy of the Articles of Organization must be filed with the secretary of state.

4. The Articles of Organization must include the following five items:

   - Name of the limited liability company.

   - Name and address of the registered agent in Minnesota.

   - A period of duration must be specified. It may not exceed 30 years.

   - List of the names and addresses of the members.

   - Must appoint "Chief Manager" and "Treasurer".

5. Required recordkeeping:

   - List of the names and addresses of all members and managers.

   - Copy of the Articles of Organization and all amendments.

   - Copies of federal, state, and local income tax returns and financial statements for the past three years.

   - Copy of the operating agreement and all amendments.

   - Any and all records determining ownership distributions of the members, and the rights of members to vote in LLC matters.

Mississippi

Mississippi's limited liability company legislation became effective on July 1, 1993. It recognizes domestic and foreign LLCs.

General Information

Address all correspondence and documentation to:

Secretary of State
P.O. Box 136
Jackson, MS 39205
(601) 359-1350

Hours: Monday through Friday, 8:00 A.M. to 5:00 P.M.

Fees:

- $25 per name reservation for 180 days.

- $50 LLC formation fee.

- No annual reporting fee.

General Formation Guidelines

1. The name of an Mississippi limited liability company must include the terms "Limited Liability Company" or the abbreviations "LLC" or "L.L.C." The name must not cause confusion with any other name on file with the secretary of state whether it be that of a corporation, limited partnership, or limited liability company.

2. Mississippi allows one person to form a limited liability company. However, please be aware that there is no certainty as to how the IRS will classify a one-member LLC.

3. One copy of the Articles of Organization must be filed with the secretary of state.

4. The Articles of Organization must include the following five items:

   - Name of the limited liability company.

   - Name and address of the registered agent in Mississippi.

   - A period of duration need not be specified.

   - List of the names and addresses of the members.

   - Statement indicating whether or not the LLC will employ managers to operate the company.

5. Required recordkeeping:

    ■ List of the names and addresses of all members and managers.

    ■ Copy of the Articles of Organization and all amendments.

    ■ Copy of the operating agreement and all amendments.

Missouri

Missouri's limited liability company legislation became effective on December 1, 1993. It recognizes domestic and foreign LLCs.

General Information

Address all correspondence and documentation to:

> Deputy Secretary of State
> Business Services
> P.O. Box 778
> Jefferson City, MO 65102
> (573) 751-3200

Hours: Monday through Friday, 8:00 A.M. to 5:00 P.M.

Fees:

■ $25 per name reservation.

■ $105 LLC formation fee.

■ No annual reporting fee.

General Formation Guidelines

1. The name of an Missouri limited liability company must include the terms "Limited Liability Company" or the abbreviations "L.L.C." or "L.C." The name must not cause confusion with any other name on file with the secretary of state whether it be that of a corporation, limited partnership, or limited liability company.

2. Missouri allows one person to form a limited liability company. However, please be aware that there is no certainty as to how the IRS will classify a one-member LLC.

3. An original and one copy of the Articles of Organization must be filed with the secretary of state.

4. The Articles of Organization must include the following six items:

   ■ Name of the limited liability company.

   ■ Purpose for the existence of the LLC.

   ■ Name and address of the registered agent in Missouri.

   ■ A period of duration must be specified.

   ■ List of the names and addresses of the members.

   ■ Statement indicating whether or not the LLC will employ managers to operate the company.

5. Required recordkeeping:

   ■ List of the names and addresses of all members and managers.

   ■ Copy of the Articles of Organization and all amendments.

   ■ Copies of federal, state, and local income tax returns and financial statements for the past three years.

   ■ Copy of the operating agreement and all amendments.

   ■ Any and all records determining ownership distributions of the members, any and all financial contributions made by the members, and the rights of members to vote in LLC matters.

Montana

Montana's limited liability company legislation became effective on October 1, 1993. It recognizes domestic and foreign LLCs.

General Information

Address all correspondence and documentation to:

Chief Corporations Bureau
State Capitol – R 225
Helena, MT 59601
(406) 444-3666

Hours: Monday through Friday, 8 A.M. to 4:30 P.M.

Fees:

- $10 per name reservation good for 120 days.

- $70 LLC formation fee.

- $10 annual reporting fee due April 15.

General Formation Guidelines

1. The name of an Montana limited liability company must include the terms "Limited Liability Company," "Limited Company" or the abbreviations "LLC", "LC", "L.L.C." or "L.C." The name must not cause confusion with any other name on file with the Chief Corporations Bureau whether it be that of a corporation, limited partnership, or limited liability company.

2. Montana allows one person to form a limited liability company. However, please be aware that there is no certainty as to how the IRS will classify a one-member LLC.

3. An original and one copy of the Articles of Organization must be filed with the Chief Corporations Bureau.

4. The Articles of Organization must include the following five items:

   - Name of the limited liability company.

   - Name and address of the registered agent in Montana.

   - A period of duration must be specified. The state imposes no limitation of the length of existence other than it cannot be perpetual.

   - List of the names and addresses of the members.

   - Statement indicating whether the LLC will be managed by the members or managers.

5. Required recordkeeping:

   - List of the names and addresses of all members and managers.

   - Copy of the Articles of Organization and all amendments.

- Copies of federal, state, and local income tax returns and financial statements for the past three years.

- Copy of the operating agreement and all amendments.

Nebraska

Nebraska's limited liability company legislation became effective on September 9, 1993. It recognizes domestic and foreign LLCs.

General Information

Address all correspondence and documentation to:

> Corporations Division
> State Capitol, #1301
> Lincoln, NE 68509
> (402) 471-4079

Hours: Monday through Friday, 8 A.M. to 5 P.M.

Fees:

- $30 per name reservation for 120 days.

- $110 LLC formation fee if initial capital does not exceed $50,000.

- No annual reporting fee.

- $10 per certified copy.

- $5 per page for documents filed (standard document is three pages).

General Formation Guidelines

1. The name of an Nebraska limited liability company must include the terms "Limited Liability Company" or the abbreviation "L.L.C." The name must not cause confusion with any other name on file with the Corporation Division whether it be that of a corporation, limited partnership, or limited liability company.

2. Nebraska allows one person to form a limited liability company, but it must be specified if the LLC will be able to add members at a later date. Please be aware that there is no certainty as to how the IRS will classify a one-member LLC.

3. An original and one copy of the Articles of Organization must be filed with the Corporations Division.

4. The Articles of Organization must include the following six items:

   ▪ Name of the limited liability company.

   ▪ Name and address of the registered agent in Nebraska.

   ▪ A period of duration of no more than 30 years.

   ▪ Listing a purpose is not required, but is recommend by the state.

   ▪ List of the names and addresses of the members.

   ▪ Statement indicating whether the LLC will be managed by the members or managers.

5. Required recordkeeping:

   ▪ List of the names and addresses of all members and managers.

   ▪ Copy of the Articles of Organization and all amendments.

   ▪ Copies of federal, state, and local income tax returns and financial statements for the past three years.

   ▪ Copy of the operating agreement and all amendments.

Nevada

Nevada's limited liability company legislation became effective on October 1, 1991. It recognizes domestic and foreign LLCs.

General Information

Address all correspondence and documentation to:

Corporations Division, LLC Division
Secretary of State
Capitol Complex
Carson City, NV 89710
(702) 687-5203

Hours: Monday through Friday, 8:00 A.M. to 5:00 P.M.

Fees:

- $20 per name reservation for 90 days.

- $125 LLC formation fee and $10 for certified copy of certificate.

- $85 annual reporting fee.

General Formation Guidelines

1. The name of a Nevada limited liability company must include the words "Limited Liability Company." The name must not cause confusion with any other name on file with the Corporations Division whether it be that of a corporation, limited partnership, or limited liability company.

2. A minimum of two members are required to form a Nevada LLC.

3. An original and one copy of the Articles of Organization must be filed with the Corporations Division.

4. The Articles of Organization must include the following five items:

    - Name of the limited liability company.

    - Name and address of the registered agent in Nevada.

    - A period of duration of no more than 30 years.

    - A statement detailing the specific purpose of the LLC.

    - List of the names and addresses of the members.

5. Required recordkeeping:

    - List of the names and addresses of all members and managers.

    - Copy of the Articles of Organization and all amendments.

    - Copies of the federal, state, and local income tax returns and financial statements for the past three years.

    - Copy of the operating agreement and all amendments.

New Hampshire

New Hampshire's limited liability company legislation became effective on July 1, 1993. It recognizes domestic and foreign LLCs.

General Information

Address all correspondence and documentation to:

> Corporations Division
> State Corporation Division
> Statehouse, Room 204
> 107 North Main Street
> Concord, NH 03301
> (603) 271-3244
> (603) 271-3246 (Name availability)

Hours: Monday through Friday, 9:00 A.M. to 5:00 P.M.

Fees:

- $15 per name reservation for 120 days.

- $85 LLC formation fee.

- $100 per year annual reporting fee.

General Formation Guidelines

1. The name of a New Hampshire limited liability company must include the term "Limited Liability Company," or the abbreviation "L.L.C." The name must not cause confusion with any other name on file with the Corporations Division whether the name be similar to the name of a corporation, a limited partnership, or a limited liability company.

2. New Hampshire allows one person to form a limited liability company, but it must be specified if the LLC will be able to add members at a later date. Please be aware that there is no certainty as to how the IRS will classify a one-member LLC.

3. An original and one copy of the Articles of Organization must be filed with the Corporations Division.

4. The Articles of Organization must include the following six items:

   - Name of the limited liability company.

   - Name and address of the registered agent in New Hampshire.

   - A period of duration of no more than 30 years.

   - Listing a purpose is not required, but it is recommended by the state.

   - List of the names and addresses of the members.

   - Statement indicating whether the LLC will be managed by the members or managers.

5. Required recordkeeping:

   - List of the names and addresses of all members and managers.

   - Copy of the Articles of Organization and all amendments.

   - Copies of the federal, state, and local income tax returns and financial statements for the past three years.

   - Copy of the operating agreement and all amendments.

New Jersey

New Jersey's limited liability company legislation became effective on January 26, 1994. It recognizes domestic and foreign LLCs.

General Information

Address all correspondence and documentation to:

> Division of Commercial Recording
> Secretary of State
> 820 Bear Tavern Road, CN308
> Trenton, NJ 08625
> (609) 530-6400

Hours: Monday through Friday, 9:00 A.M. to 5:00 P.M.

Fees:

- $50 per name reservation for 120 days.

- $100 LLC formation fee plus $10 to expedite filing.

- No required annual reporting fee. See below.

General Formation Guidelines

1. The name of a New Jersey limited liability company must include the term "Limited Liability Company" or the abbreviation "L.L.C." The name must not cause confusion with any other name on file with the secretary of state whether it be that of a corporation, limited partnership, or limited liability company.

2. Two or more people are required to form a New Jersey LLC.

3. A signed original copy of the Articles of Organization must be sent to the Division of Commercial Recording.

4. The Articles of Organization must include the following three items:

   - Name of the limited liability company.

   - Name and address of the registered agent in New Jersey.

   - Period of duration if not perpetual.

5. Required recordkeeping:

   - A written operating agreement is required but is not made public. The state imposes no recordkeeping requirements and does not require LLCs to distribute regular reports to its members. The LLC should maintain minutes of the meetings of the members and managers of the company, however, and should also keep a copy of the operating agreement.

New Mexico

New Mexico's limited liability company legislation became effective on June 18, 1993. It recognizes domestic and foreign LLCs.

General Information

Address all correspondence and documentation to:

Office of the New Mexico State Corporation Commission
P.O. Drawer 1269
Santa Fe, NM 87504-1269
(505) 827-4504
(505) 827-4504 (Name availability)

Hours: Monday through Friday, 8:00 A.M. to 5:00 P.M.

Fees:

- $20 per name reservation for 120 days.

- $50 LLC formation fee.

- No required annual reporting fee. See below.

General Formation Guidelines

1. The name of a New Mexico limited liability company must include the terms "Limited Liability Company" or "A Limited Company" or the abbreviations "LLC", "L.L.C.", "LC", or "L.C." The words "Limited" and "Company" may be abbreviated "Ltd." and "Co." respectively. The name must not cause confusion with any other name on file with the State Corporation Commission whether it be that of a corporation, limited partnership, or limited liability company.

2. New Mexico allows one person to form a limited liability company. However, please be aware that there is no certainty as to how the IRS will classify a one-member LLC.

3. An original and one copy of the Articles of Organization must be filed with the State Corporation Commission.

4. The Articles of Organization must include the following four items:

   - Name of the limited liability company.

   - Name and address of the registered agent in New Mexico.

   - Period of duration if not perpetual.

- Statement indicating whether or not the LLC will employ managers to operate the company.

5. Required recordkeeping:

   - A written operating agreement is required but is not made public.

   - The state imposes no recordkeeping requirements and does not require LLCs to distribute regular reports to its members.

   - The LLC should maintain minutes of the meetings of the members and managers of the company, however, and should also keep a copy of the operating agreement.

New York

New York's limited liability company legislation became effective on October 24, 1994. It recognizes domestic and foreign LLCs.

General Information

Address all correspondence and documentation to:

Secretary of State
162 Washington Avenue
Albany, NY 12231
(518) 474-4750

Hours: Monday through Friday, 9:00 A.M. to 5:00 P.M.

Fees:

- $20 per name reservation for 60 days.

- $200 LLC formation fee. A $10 certified copy is suggested.

- Up to $1,800 for required publication of LLC formation notice. See below.

- $9 annual reporting fee.

General Formation Guidelines

1. The name of a New York limited liability company must include the term "Limited Liability Company" or the abbreviations "LLC" or "L.L.C." The name must not cause confusion with any other name on file with the secretary of state whether it be that of a corporation, limited partnership, or limited liability company. The New York Limited Liability Company Law (NYLLCL) also lists many specific terms and phrases that may not be used. Obtain a copy of the NYLLCL manual before selecting a name.

2. New York allows one person to form an LLC. However, please be aware that there is no certainty as to how the IRS will classify a one-member LLC.

3. An original of the Articles of Organization must be filed with the secretary of state.

   ■ The Articles of Organization must include the following seven items:

   ■ Name of the limited liability company.

   ■ Principal office address, including its county.

   ■ Statement that the secretary of state is the agent for service of process to which correspondence and documentation are sent.

   ■ Statement indicating whether or not members are liable for LLC's debts.

   ■ Period of duration if not perpetual.

   ■ Statement indicating whether or not the LLC will employ managers to operate the company.

   ■ Name and address of the registered agent in New York.

5. Required recordkeeping:

   ■ List of the names and addresses of all members and managers.

   ■ List of members' cash and other contributions and their allocations of profits and/or losses.

   ■ Copy of the Articles of Organization.

- Copies of federal, state, and local income tax returns for the past three years.

- Copy of the operating agreement and all amendments.

6. New York requires a published notice for newly formed LLCs. The notice must be filed in two publications once a week for six successive weeks and may cost up to $1,800 depending on the county.

North Carolina

North Carolina's limited liability company legislation became effective on October 1, 1993. It recognizes domestic and foreign LLCs.

General Information

Address all correspondence and documentation to:

Corporations Division
Secretary of State
300 North Salisbury Street
Raleigh, NC 27603-5909
(919) 733-4201

Hours: Monday through Friday, 9:00 A.M. to 5:00 P.M.

Fees:

- $10 per name reservation for 120 days.

- $100 LLC formation fee.

- $200 annual reporting fee.

General Formation Guidelines

1. The name of a North Carolina limited liability company must include the terms "Limited Liability Company", "Ltd. Liability Co.", "Limited Liability Co.", "Ltd. Liability Company", or the abbreviations "LLC" or "L.L.C." The name must not cause confusion with any other name on file with the secretary of state whether it be that of a corporation, limited partnership, or limited liability company.

2. Two or more people are required to form a North Carolina LLC.

3. An original and one copy of the Articles of Organization must be filed with the Corporations Division.

4. The Articles of Organization must include the following four items:

   ■ Name of the limited liability company.

   ■ Name and address of the registered agent in North Carolina.

   ■ Period of duration if not perpetual.

   ■ Name and address of each organizer. At least two organizers are required.

5. Required recordkeeping:

   ■ List of the names and addresses of all members.

   ■ Copy of the Articles of Organization.

   ■ Copies of federal, state, and local income tax returns and financial statements for the past five years.

   ■ Copy of operating agreement and all amendments.

   ■ Any other information about the LLC "as is just and reasonable."

North Dakota

North Dakota's limited liability company legislation became effective on July 1, 1993. It recognizes domestic and foreign LLCs.

General Information

Address all correspondence and documentation to:

Secretary of State
State of North Dakota
600 East Boulevard Avenue
Bismarck, ND 58505-0500
(701) 328-2900
(701) 328-4284 (Name availability)

Hours: Monday through Friday, 8:00 A.M. to 5:00 P.M.

Fees:

- $10 per name reservation for twelve months.

- $5 per name search.

- $135 LLC formation fee.

- $25 annual reporting fee due August 1.

General Formation Guidelines

1. The name of a North Dakota limited liability company must include the terms "Limited Liability Company" or the abbreviation "L.L.C." The name must not cause confusion with any other name on file with the secretary of state whether it be that of a corporation, limited partnership, or limited liability company.

2. Two or more people are required to form a North Dakota LLC.

3. An original and one copy of the Articles of Organization must be filed with the secretary of state.

4. The Articles of Organization must include the following six items:

   - Name of the limited liability company.

   - Principal office address.

   - Name and address of the registered agent in North Dakota.

   - Period of duration if not perpetual.

   - Names and addresses of each organizer.

   - Statement indicating whether or not members have the power to avoid LLC dissolution by agreeing to a dissolution avoidance consent.

5. Required recordkeeping:

   - List of the names and addresses of all members.

   - List of members' cash and other contributions to the LLC, as well as disclosure and record of all contributions.

   - Copy of the Articles of Organization and all amendments.

- Copies of federal, state, and local income tax returns and financial statements for past three years.

- Minutes of all members' meetings for the last three years.

Ohio

Ohio's limited liability company legislation became effective on July 1, 1994. It recognizes domestic and foreign LLCs.

General Information

Address all correspondence and documentation to:

Corporation Division
Ohio Secretary of State
30 East Broad Street
Columbus, OH 43215
(614) 466-3910

Hours: Monday through Friday, 8:30 A.M. to 5:00 P.M.

Fees:

- $5 per name reservation for 60 days.

- $85 LLC formation fee.

- No annual reporting fee. See below.

General Formation Guidelines

1. The name of an Ohio limited liability company must include the term "Limited Liability Company" or the abbreviations "Limited", "Ltd.", or "ltd." The name must not cause confusion with any other name on file with the secretary of state whether it be that of a corporation, limited partnership, or limited liability company.

2. Two or more people are required to form an Ohio LLC.

3. An original and one copy of the Articles of Organization must be filed with the Corporation Division. The filing must include a statement of appointment of the registered agent signed by a

majority of the LLC members as well as the agent's written acceptance of the appointment.

4. The Articles of Organization must include the following three items:

    ■ Name of the limited liability company.

    ■ Period of duration if not perpetual.

    ■ Address to which interested parties may direct requests for copies of the operating agreement and by-laws.

5. Required recordkeeping:

    ■ Ohio LLCs are not required to file annual reports with the secretary of state. However, the LLC should keep:

        ■ List of the names and addresses of all members.

        ■ List of members' cash and other contribution to the LLC.

        ■ Copy of the Articles of Organization and amendments.

        ■ Copies of federal, state, and local income tax returns for the past three years.

        ■ Copy of the operating agreement and all amendments.

Oklahoma

Oklahoma's limited liability company legislation became effective on September 1, 1992. It recognizes domestic and foreign LLCs.

General Information

Address all correspondence and documentation to:

> Secretary of State
> 2300 North Lincoln Blvd., Room 101
> State Capitol Building
> Oklahoma City, OK 73105
> (405) 521-3911

Hours: Monday through Friday, 8:00 A.M. to 5:00 P.M.

Fees:

- $10 per name reservation for 60 days.

- $100 LLC formation fee.

- No annual reporting fee. See below.

General Formation Guidelines

1. The name of an Oklahoma limited liability company must include the terms "Limited Liability Company" or "Limited Company" or the abbreviations "L.L.C." or "L.C." The name must not cause confusion with any other name on file with the secretary of state whether it be that of a corporation, limited partnership, or limited liability company.

2. Two or more people are required to form an Oklahoma LLC.

3. Two original copies of the Articles of Organization must be filed with the secretary of state.

4. The Articles of Organization must include the following four items:

   - Name of the limited liability company.

   - Principal office address.

   - Name and address of the registered agent in Oklahoma.

   - Period of duration if not perpetual.

5. Required recordkeeping:

   - Oklahoma LLCs are not required to file annual reports with the secretary of state. However, the LLC should keep:

     - List of the names and addresses of all past and present members and managers.

     - Articles of Organization and all amendments.

     - Copies of federal, state, and local income tax returns for the past three years.

     - Documentation of members' voting rights.

Oregon

Oregon's limited liability company legislation became effective on January 1, 1994. It recognizes domestic and foreign LLCs.

General Information

Address all correspondence and documentation to:

Corporation Division
Office of the Secretary of State
255 Capitol St. N.E., Suite 151
Salem, OR 97310-1327
(503) 986-2200

Hours: Monday through Friday, 8:00 A.M. to 5:00 P.M.

Fees:

- $10 per name reservation for 120 days.

- $40 LLC formation fee.

- $30 annual reporting fee.

General Formation Guidelines

1. The name of an Oregon limited liability company must include the term "Limited Liability Company" or the abbreviation "L.L.C." The name must not cause confusion with any other name on file with the secretary of state whether it be that of a corporation, limited partnership, or limited liability company.

2. Oregon allows one person to form a LLC. However, please be aware that there is no certainty as to how the IRS will classify a one-member LLC.

3. Two original copies of the Articles of Organization must be filed with the Corporation Division.

4. The Articles of Organization must include the following five items:

   - Name of the limited liability company.

   - Name and address of the registered agent in Oregon.

- Period of duration if not perpetual.

- Names and addresses of each organizer.

- Statement indicating whether or not the LLC will employ managers to operate the company.

5. Required recordkeeping:

    - List of the names and addresses of all members and managers.

    - Name of the LLC and state under whose law it was organized.

    - Current registered agent and address.

    - Principal business office address.

    - Federal tax I.D. number.

Pennsylvania

Pennsylvania's limited liability company legislation became effective on February 6, 1995. It recognizes domestic and foreign LLCs.

General Information

Address all correspondence and documentation to:

> Department of State
> Corporations Bureau
> P.O. Box 8722
> Harrisburg, PA 17105-8722
> (717) 787-6271

Hours: Monday through Friday, 8:00 A.M. to 5:00 P.M.

Fees:

- $52 per name reservation for 120 days.

- $100 LLC formation fee.

- Annual fee of $200 multiplied by the number of members in the LLC.

General Formation Guidelines

1. The name of the Pennsylvania limited liability company must include the term "Limited Liability Company" or the abbreviations "LLC" or "L.L.C." The name must not cause confusion with any other name on file with the Corporations Bureau whether it be that of a corporation, limited partnership, or limited liability company.

2. Pennsylvania allows one person to form a limited liability company, but it must be specified if the LLC will be able to add members at a later date. Please be aware that there is no certainty as to how the IRS will classify a one-member LLC.

3. An original and one copy of the Articles of Organization must be filed with the Corporations Division.

4. The Articles of Organization must include the following five items:

   ■ Name of the limited liability company.

   ■ Name and address of the registered agent in Pennsylvania.

   ■ A period of duration which may be perpetual.

   ■ Listing a purpose is only required for professional LLCs.

   ■ List of the names and addresses of the members.

5. Required recordkeeping:

   ■ List of the names and addresses of all members.

   ■ Copy of the Articles of Organization and all amendments.

   ■ Copy of the operating agreement and all amendments.

Rhode Island

Rhode Island's limited liability company legislation became effective on September 21, 1992. It recognizes domestic and foreign LLCs.

General Information

Address all correspondence and documentation to:

Corporation Division
Secretary of State
100 North Main Street
Providence, RI 02903
(401) 277-3040

Hours: Monday through Friday, 8:30 A.M. to 4:30 P.M.

Fees:

- $50 per name reservation for 120 days.

- $150 LLC formation fee.

- $50 required annual reporting fee between September 1 and November 1.

General Formation Guidelines

1. The name of a Rhode Island limited liability company must include the term "Limited Liability Company" or the abbreviations "LLC" or "L.L.C." The name must not cause confusion with any other name on file with the secretary of state whether it be that of a corporation, limited partnership, or limited liability company.

2. Two or more people are required to form a Rhode Island LLC.

3. Two original copies of the Articles of Organization must be filed with the Corporations Division.

4. The Articles of Organization must include the following six items:

   - Name of the limited liability company.

   - Principal office address.

   - Name and address of the registered agent in Rhode Island.

   - Period of duration if not perpetual.

   - Statement that there are at least two members.

   - Statement of tax treatment — partnership or corporation.

5. Required recordkeeping:

   ■ List of the names and addresses of all members and managers.

   ■ Copy of the Articles of Organization and all amendments.

   ■ Copies of federal, state, and local income tax returns for the past five years.

South Carolina

South Carolina's limited liability company legislation became effective on June 16, 1994. It recognizes domestic and foreign LLCs.

General Information

Address all correspondence and documentation to:

Secretary of State
Edgar Brown Building
P.O. Box 11350
Columbia, SC 29211
(803) 734-2158

Hours: Monday through Friday, 8:00 A.M. to 5:00 P.M.

Fees:

■ $10 per name reservation for 120 days.

■ $110 LLC formation fee.

■ No annual reporting fee.

General Formation Guidelines

1. The name of a South Carolina limited liability company must include the terms "Limited Liability Company" or "Limited Company" or the abbreviations "L.L.C.", "L.C.", "LC", or "L.C." "Limited" and "Company" may be abbreviated "Ltd." and "Co." respectively. The name must not cause confusion with any other name on file with the secretary of state whether it be that of a corporation, limited partnership, or limited liability company.

2. Two or more people are required to form a South Carolina LLC.

3. Two original copies of the Articles of Organization must be filed with the secretary of state.

4. The Articles of Organization must include the following five items:

   - Name of the limited liability company.

   - Name and address of the registered agent in South Carolina.

   - Period of duration if not perpetual.

   - Names and signatures of the initial members.

   - Statement indicating whether or not the LLC will employ managers to operate the company.

5. Required recordkeeping:

   - List of the names and addresses of all members and managers.

   - Copy of the Articles of Organization and all amendments.

   - Copies of federal, state, and local income tax returns for the past six years.

   - Copy of the operating agreement and all amendments.

South Dakota

South Dakota's limited liability company legislation became effective on July 1, 1993. It recognizes domestic and foreign LLCs.

General Information

Address all correspondence and documentation to:

Secretary of State
Capitol Building, 2nd Floor
500 East Capitol
Pierre, SD 57501
(605) 773-4845

Hours: Monday through Friday, 8:00 A.M. to 5:00 P.M.

Fees:

- $10 per name reservation for 120 days.

- LLC formation fee is based on the initial capital: minimum $50 for up to $50,000; $100 for $50,001 to $100,000; and $100 plus $0.50 for each additional $1,000 above $100,000.

- $50 annual reporting fee.

General Formation Guidelines

1. The name of a South Dakota limited liability company must include the term "Limited Liability Company" or the abbreviation "L.L.C." The name must not cause confusion with any other name on file with the secretary of state whether it be that of a corporation, limited partnership, or limited liability company.

2. Two or more people are required to form a South Dakota LLC.

3. Two original copies of the Articles of Organization must be filed with the secretary of state.

4. The Articles of Organization must include the following eight items:

    - Name of the limited liability company.

    - Purpose for which the LLC was formed.

    - Name and address of the registered agent in South Dakota.

    - Period of duration if not perpetual.

    - Description of members' cash and other contributions.

    - Terms and conditions for admitting new members.

    - Terms and conditions for continuing business after the termination of a member.

    - Statement indicating whether or not the LLC will employ managers to operate the company.

5. Required recordkeeping:

    - List of the names and addresses of all members and managers.

    - Copy of the Articles of Organization and all amendments.

- Copies of federal, state, and local income tax returns and financial statements for the past three years.

- Copy of the operating agreement and all amendments.

Tennessee

Tennessee's limited liability company legislation became effective on June 21, 1994. It recognizes domestic and foreign LLCs.

General Information

Address all correspondence and documentation to:

Secretary of State
James K. Polk Building, Suite 1800
Nashville, TN 37243-0306
(615) 741-4994

Hours: Monday through Friday, 8:30 A.M. to 5:00 P.M.

Fees:

- $10 per name reservation for four months.

- $300 LLC formation fee for six or fewer members and $50 per member for more than six members.

- $300 annual reporting fee. Fee and report due on the first day of the fourth month following the close of the LLC's fiscal year.

- $20 county recording fee.

General Formation Guidelines

1. The name of a Tennessee limited liability company must include the term "Limited Liability Company" or the abbreviations "LLC" or "L.L.C." The name must not cause confusion with any other name on file with the secretary of state whether it be that of a corporation, limited partnership, or limited liability company.

2. Two or more people are required to form a Tennessee LLC.

3. Two original copies of the Articles of Organization must be filed with the secretary of state.

4. The Articles of Organization must include the following eight items:

   - Name of the limited liability company.

   - Principal office address, including its county.

   - Name and address of the registered agent in Tennessee.

   - Period of duration if not perpetual.

   - Names and addresses for each organizer.

   - Statement indicating that, at the time of formation, there are two or more members and specifying the total number of members at the time of filing.

   - Statement indicating whether or not the LLC will employ managers to operate the company.

   - Statement indicating whether or not the LLC has the power to expel members.

5. Required recordkeeping:

   - List of the names and addresses of all members and managers.

   - List of all assignees of financial rights and a description of rights assigned.

   - Copy of the Articles of Organization and all amendments.

   - Copy of the operating agreement and all amendments.

   - Copies of federal, state, and local income tax returns and financial statements for the past three years.

   - Records of all proceedings, if any.

   - Records of all proceedings of the Board of Governors, if any.

   - Copy of the limited liability company's most recent annual report.

Texas

Texas's limited liability company legislation became effective on August 26, 1992, and was significantly amended in 1993. It recognizes domestic and foreign LLCs.

General Information

Address all correspondence and documentation to:

> Statutory Filings Division
> Secretary of State
> Corporations Section
> P.O. Box 13697
> Austin, TX 78711-3697
> (512) 463-5583

Hours: Monday through Friday, 8:00 A.M. to 5:00 P.M.

Fees:

- $25 per name reservation for 120 days.

- $200 LLC formation fee ($10 additional for special handling).

- Annual reporting fee based on amount capitalized or surplus income due May 15.

General Formation Guidelines

1. The name of a Texas limited liability company must include the term "Limited Liability Company" or "Limited Company" or the abbreviations "L.L.C.", "LLC", "LC", or "L.C." "Limited" and "Company" may be abbreviated "Ltd." and "Co." respectively. The name must not cause confusion with any other name on file with the secretary of state whether it be that of a corporation, limited partnership, or limited liability company.

2. Texas allows one person to form an LLC. However, please be aware that there is no certainty as to how the IRS will classify a one-member LLC.

3. An original and one copy of the Articles of Organization must be filed with the Statutory Filings Division.

4. The Articles of Organization must include all of the following six items:

   ■ Name of the limited liability company.

   ■ Purpose for which the LLC was formed.

   ■ Name and address of the registered agent in Texas.

   ■ Period of duration if not perpetual.

   ■ List of the names and addresses of all managers and members.

   ■ Names and addresses of each organizer.

5. Required recordkeeping:

   ■ List of the names and addresses of all members and managers.

   ■ List of members' cash and other contributions.

   ■ Copies of federal, state, and local income tax returns for the past six years.

   ■ Copy of the Articles of Organization and all amendments.

Utah

Utah's limited liability company legislation became effective on July 1, 1991, and was amended in 1992 and 1994. It recognizes domestic and foreign LLCs.

General Information

Address all correspondence and documentation to:

> Division of Corporations
> Department of Commerce
> P.O. Box 45801
> Salt Lake City, UT 84145-0801
> (801) 530-4849

Hours: Monday through Friday, 8:00 A.M. to 5:00 P.M.

Fees

- $20 per name reservation for 120 days.

- $75 LLC formation fee.

- $15 required annual reporting fee and report due within one month of the anniversary date of the company's formation.

General Formation Guidelines

1. The name of a Utah limited liability company must include the term "Limited Liability Company" or "Limited Company" or the abbreviations "L.L.C.", "LLC", "LC", or "L.C." The name must not cause confusion with any other name on file with the Department of Commerce whether it be that of a corporation, limited partnership, or limited liability company.

2. Two or more people are required to form a Utah LLC.

3. An original and one copy of the Articles of Organization must be filed with the Division of Corporations.

4. The Articles of Organization must include the following six items:

   - Name of the limited liability company.

   - Purpose for which the LLC was formed.

   - Name and address of the registered agent in Utah.

   - Period of duration if not perpetual.

   - List of the names and addresses of all members and managers.

   - Signatures from at least two members or managers along with the signature of the registered agent.

5. Required recordkeeping:

   - List of the names and addresses of all members and managers.

   - List of members' cash or other contributions.

   - Copy of the Articles of Organization and all amendments.

   - Copies of federal, state, and local income tax returns and financial statements for the past three years.

Vermont

Vermont's limited liability company legislation became effective July 1, 1996. It recognizes both domestic and foreign LLCs.

General Information

Address all correspondence and documentation to:

> Corporations Division
> Secretary of State
> Pavilion Office Building
> Montpelier, VT 05602-2710
> (802) 828-2386

Hours: Monday through Friday, 8:00 A.M. to 5:00 P.M.

Fees:

- $25 per name reservation for.

- $75 LLC domestic formation fee.

- $100 LLC foreign formation fee.

- $25 annual reporting fee.

Annual Report must be filed between October 1 and December 31st for the next calendar year.

General Formation Guidelines

1. The name of a Vermont limited liability company must include the terms "Limited Company," "Limited Liability Company" or the abbreviations "LLC", "LC", "Ltd. Co." The name must not cause confusion with any other name on file with the state Corporations Division whether it be that of a corporation, limited partnership or limited liability company.

2. The effective date of the LLC provision can be delayed up to 90 days from the original date of filing.

3. The state does not have a minimum requirement of members to form a LLC.

4. The Articles of Organization must include the following five items:

- Principal office address.

- Name and address of the Registered Agent in Vermont.

- Period of duration if not perpetual (up to 30 years).

- Filing must be typewritten.

- Must be filed in duplicate.

5. Required recordkeeping:

   - List of the names and addresses of all members and managers.

   - Copy of the Articles of Organization and all amendments.

   - Copies of federal, state, and local income tax returns and financial statements for the past three years.

   - Copies of the operating agreement for the past three years.

Virginia

Virginia's limited liability company legislation became effective on July 1, 1991, and was amended in 1994. It recognizes domestic and foreign LLCs.

General Information

Address all correspondence and documentation to:

> Office of the Clerk
> State Corporation Commission
> 1300 East Main Street
> Richmond, VA 23218
> (804) 371-9733

Hours: Monday through Friday, 8:15 A.M. to 5:00 P.M.

Fees:

- $10 per name reservation for 120 days.

- $100 LLC formation fee.

- $50 annual reporting fee.

- $6 certified copy.

General Formation Guidelines

1. The name of a Virginia limited liability company must include the terms "Limited Liability Company" or "Limited Company" or the abbreviations "L.L.C." or "L.C." The name must not cause confusion with any other name on file with the State Corporation Commission whether it be that of a corporation, limited partnership, or limited liability company.

2. Virginia allows one person to form an LLC. However, please be aware that there is no certainty as to how the IRS will classify a one-member LLC.

3. An original Articles of Organization must be filed with the Office of the Clerk.

4. The Articles of Organization must include the following five items:

   - Name of the limited liability company.

   - Principal office address.

   - Name and address of the registered agent in Virginia.

   - Period of duration if not perpetual.

   - Signature of organizer.

5. Required recordkeeping:

   - List of the names and addresses of all members and managers.

   - Copy of the Articles of Organization and all amendments.

   - Copies of federal, state, and local income tax returns and financial statements for the past three years

   - Copies of the operating agreement for the past three years.

Washington

Washington's limited liability company legislation became effective on October 1, 1994. It recognizes domestic and foreign LLCs.

General Information

Address all correspondence and documentation to:

Corporations Division
Office of the Secretary of State
P.O. Box 40234
Olympia, WA 98504-0234
(360) 753-7115

Hours: Monday through Friday, 8:00 A.M. to 5:00 P.M.

Fees:

- $30 per name reservation for 180 days.

- $175 LLC formation fee.

- $59 required annual reporting fee.

General Formation Guidelines

1. The name of a Washington limited liability company must include the terms "Limited Liability Company" or "Limited Company" or the abbreviation "L.L.C." The word "Company" may be abbreviated "Co." The name must not cause confusion with any other name on file with the secretary of state whether it be that of a corporation, limited partnership, or limited liability company.

2. Two or more people are required to form a Washington LLC.

3. An original and a copy of the Articles of Organization must be filed with the Corporations Division.

4. The Articles of Organization must include the following six items:

   - Name of the limited liability company.

   - Principal business address.

   - Name and address of the registered agent in Washington.

   - Period of duration if not perpetual.

   - Names and addresses of people executing the Articles of Organization. They do not have to be members or managers of the LLC.

   - Statement indicating whether or not the LLC will employ managers to operate the company.

5. Required recordkeeping:

    ■ List of the names and addresses of all past and present members and managers.

    ■ List of members' cash and other contributions.

    ■ Copy of the Articles of Organization and all amendments.

    ■ Copies of federal, state, and local income tax returns and financial statements for the past three years.

    ■ Copy of the operating agreement with all amendments.

West Virginia

West Virginia's limited liability company legislation became effective on March 6, 1992. It recognizes domestic and foreign LLCs.

General Information

Address all correspondence and documentation to:

> Corporate Division
> Secretary of State
> State Capitol Building, Room W-139
> Charleston, WV 25305
> (304) 558-8000

Hours: Monday through Friday, 8:30 A.M. to 4:30 P.M.

Fees:

■ $5 per name reservation for 120 days.

■ $10 LLC formation fee.

■ No annual reporting fee. See below.

General Formation Guidelines

1. The name of a West Virginia limited liability company must include the term "Limited Liability Company." The name must not cause confusion with any other name on file with the secretary of state whether it be that of a corporation, limited partnership, or limited liability company.

2. Two or more people are required to form a West Virginia LLC.

3. Two original copies of the Articles of Organization must be filed with the Corporate Division.

4. The Articles of Organization must include the following six items:

   ■ Name of the limited liability company.

   ■ Principal office address in West Virginia.

   ■ Purpose for which the LLC was formed.

   ■ Name and address of the registered agent in West Virginia.

   ■ Names and address of the initial members.

   ■ Signature of member authorized to sign for the LLC.

5. Required recordkeeping:

   ■ West Virginia imposes no recordkeeping requirements.

   ■ West Virginia does not require LLCs to distribute regular reports to its members.

   ■ The LLC should maintain minutes of the meetings of the members and managers of the company, however, and should also keep a copy of the operating agreement.

Wisconsin

Wisconsin's limited liability company legislation became effective on January 1, 1994. It recognizes domestic and foreign LLCs.

General Information

Address all correspondence and documentation to:

> Department of Financial Institutions
> Division of Corporate and Customer Services
> P.O. Box 7846
> Madison, WI 53703-7846
> (608) 266-3590

Hours: Monday through Friday, 7:45 A.M. to 4:30 P.M.

Fees:

- $30 per name reservation placed by telephone, $15 if reserved by mail for 120 days.

- $130 LLC formation fee.

- No annual reporting fee.

General Formation Guidelines

1. The name of an Wisconsin limited liability company must include the terms "Limited Liability Company" or the abbreviations "LLC" or "L.L.C." The word "Company" may be abbreviated to "Co." The name must not cause confusion with any other name on file with the Corporations Division whether it be that of a corporation, limited partnership, or limited liability company.

2. Two or more people are required to form a Wisconsin LLC.

3. An original and one copy of the Articles of Organization must be filed with the Corporations Division.

4. The Articles of Organization must include the following four items:

   - Name of the limited liability company.

   - Name and address of the registered agent in Wisconsin.

   - List of the names and addresses of the members.

   - If the LLC will have managers, that must be stated in the Articles.

5. Required recordkeeping:

   - Records of LLC must be maintained at the principal office address.

   - List of the names and addresses of all members and managers.

   - Copy of the Articles of Organization and all amendments.

   - Copies of federal, state, and local income tax returns and financial statements for the past three years.

   - Copy of the operating agreement and all amendments.

Wyoming

Wyoming's limited liability company legislation became effective in 1977. It recognizes domestic and foreign LLCs.

General Information

Address all correspondence and documentation to:

Office of the Secretary of State
Capitol Building
Cheyenne, WY 82002
(307) 777-7378
(307) 777-7311 (Name availability)

Hours: Monday through Friday, 8 A.M. to 5 P.M.

Fees:

- $30 per name reservation for 120 days.

- $100 LLC formation fee for companies capitalized from $0 to $50,000; $200 for companies capitalized from $50,001 to $100,000; $200 plus $1 for each $1,000 over $100,000 capitalization. The total fee is not to exceed $25,000.

- $100 annual reporting fee.

General Formation Guidelines

1. The name of a Wyoming limited liability company must include the terms "Limited Liability Company" or the abbreviations "LLC" or "L.L.C." The word "Company" may be abbreviated to "Co." The name must not cause confusion with any other name on file with the secretary of state whether it be that of a corporation, limited partnership, or limited liability company.

2. Two or more people are required to form a Wyoming LLC.

3. An original and one copy of the Articles of Organization must be filed with the secretary of state.

4. The Articles of Organization must include the following six items:

   - Name of the limited liability company.

- Name and address of the registered agent in Wyoming.

- Any purpose for existence is authorized except banking and/or insurance.

- Period of duration of the LLC, not to exceed 30 years.

- List of the names and addresses of the members.

- A statement indicating whether the LLC will be managed by members of managers.

5. Required recordkeeping:

- The state imposes no recordkeeping requirements and does not require LLCs to distribute regular reports to its members.

- The LLC should maintain minutes of the meetings of the members and managers of the company, however, and should also keep a copy of the operating agreement.

State Forms

The following forms are reproductions of state forms provided by various state agencies for your reference. Obtain official copies of the forms from the appropriate state agency prior to filing in your state.

The form you receive from your state may not be an exact duplicate because of potential updates. Listed below are the pages your state's forms begin on.

Alabama Form

INFORMATION ON FORMING A LIMITED LIABILITY COMPANY
UNDER THE ALASKA LIMITED LIABILITY ACT

On June 8, 1994 the Alaska Limited Liability Act was signed into law. The effective date for the Act is July 1, 1995.

To determine the tax liability of a Limited Liability Company, the Internal Revenue Service looks at four characteristics of the formed LLC:

1. the limited liability of the members or manager;

2. the ability of the LLC to freely continue its existence upon the death, insanity, bankruptcy, retirement, resignation, or expulsion of any of its members;

3. centralization of management of the LLC; and

4. the ability of the members to freely transfer their right to participate in the affairs of the LLC to another person.

If the formed LLC meets one or two of these characteristics, it will be treated as a partnership for tax purposes. If the LLC meets more than two of these characteristics, it will be treated as a corporation for tax purposes by the state and the IRS.

When organizing an LLC, Alaska's Act allows members to choose characteristics which best fit the business purposes of the entity. It is assumed that most persons forming an LLC will desire to form in such a manner as to receive the more favorable tax treatment of a partnership. Since limited liability is a default provision of the Act, **extreme caution must be exercised in drafting the articles of organization** to avoid adopting characteristics which would cause the LLC to be treated as a corporation for tax purposes.

IF YOU REQUIRE ADDITIONAL ASSISTANCE IN COMPLETING ARTICLES OF ORGANIZATION, OR ARE UNCLEAR OF THE TAX LIABILITIES INVOLVED, YOU ARE STRONGLY ADVISED TO SEEK THE SERVICES OF AN ATTORNEY OR CERTIFIED PUBLIC ACCOUNTANT. THE DIVISION IS PROHIBITED FROM RESPONDING TO QUESTIONS REGARDING THESE MATTERS.

An operating agreement is not required to be submitted with articles of organization, therefore the Division will not file operating agreements. However, members of an LLC are encouraged to adopt and maintain an operating agreement relating to the management and regulation of the business affairs of the LLC. The articles of organization may restrict or eliminate the power of members to adopt, amend, or repeal an operating agreement.

INSTRUCTIONS ON FILING ARTICLES OF ORGANIZATION

Two or more persons may form a Limited Liability Company by signing and delivering to the Division an original and exact copy of Articles of Organization.

The submitted documents must be in dark, legible print on paper which is no larger than 8 1/2 by 11 inches. The articles should contain a statement that they are being filed under the provisions of the Alaska Limited Liability Act.

The fee for submitting Articles of Organization is $250.00 ($150.00 filing fee plus a biennial license fee of $100.00).

08-430 (Rev. 6/95)

Alaska Form

INFORMATION ON FORMING A LIMITED LIABILITY COMPANY
UNDER THE ALASKA LIMITED LIABILITY ACT

On June 8, 1994 the Alaska Limited Liability Act was signed into law. The effective date for the Act is July 1, 1995.

To determine the tax liability of a Limited Liability Company, the Internal Revenue Service looks at four characteristics of the formed LLC:

1. the limited liability of the members or manager;

2. the ability of the LLC to freely continue its existence upon the death, insanity, bankruptcy, retirement, resignation, or expulsion of any of its members;

3. centralization of management of the LLC; and

4. the ability of the members to freely transfer their right to participate in the affairs of the LLC to another person.

If the formed LLC meets one or two of these characteristics, it will be treated as a partnership for tax purposes. If the LLC meets more than two of these characteristics, it will be treated as a corporation for tax purposes by the state and the IRS.

When organizing an LLC, Alaska's Act allows members to choose characteristics which best fit the business purposes of the entity. It is assumed that most persons forming an LLC will desire to form in such a manner as to receive the more favorable tax treatment of a partnership. Since limited liability is a default provision of the Act, **extreme caution must be exercised in drafting the articles of organization** to avoid adopting characteristics which would cause the LLC to be treated as a corporation for tax purposes.

IF YOU REQUIRE ADDITIONAL ASSISTANCE IN COMPLETING ARTICLES OF ORGANIZATION, OR ARE UNCLEAR OF THE TAX LIABILITIES INVOLVED, YOU ARE STRONGLY ADVISED TO SEEK THE SERVICES OF AN ATTORNEY OR CERTIFIED PUBLIC ACCOUNTANT. THE DIVISION IS PROHIBITED FROM RESPONDING TO QUESTIONS REGARDING THESE MATTERS.

An operating agreement is not required to be submitted with articles of organization, therefore the Division will not file operating agreements. However, members of an LLC are encouraged to adopt and maintain an operating agreement relating to the management and regulation of the business affairs of the LLC. The articles of organization may restrict or eliminate the power of members to adopt, amend, or repeal an operating agreement.

INSTRUCTIONS ON FILING ARTICLES OF ORGANIZATION

Two or more persons may form a Limited Liability Company by signing and delivering to the Division an original and exact copy of Articles of Organization.

The submitted documents must be in dark, legible print on paper which is no larger than 8 1/2 by 11 inches. The articles should contain a statement that they are being filed under the provisions of the Alaska Limited Liability Act.

The fee for submitting Articles of Organization is $250.00 ($150.00 filing fee plus a biennial license fee of $100.00).

08-430 (Rev. 6/95)

Alaska Form (continued)

Effective July 1, 1995, Alaska Statute 10.50.075 requires that the articles of organization set out:

1. **The name of the limited liability company.** The name must contain the words "limited liability company," or the abbreviation LLC. The name may not contain the words "city" or "borough," or otherwise imply that the company is a municipality. The name must be distinguishable from trade names on record with the Division of Banking, Securities, and Corporations.

2. **The purpose for which the LLC is organized,** and a list of the standard industrial classification (S.I.C.) codes that best describe its activities (see S.I.C. code list attached)

3. **The name, mailing address, and physical address** (if different from the mailing address) of the LLC's registered agent. The agent must be an individual or a corporation authorized to transact business in this state.

4. **If applicable, the latest date or event** which will cause the LLC to cease to exist.

5. **Whether the business affairs of the LLC** are to be conducted by the members or by a manager, and the names and addresses of those members or the manager (names and addresses optional).

6. **If applicable, the terms and conditions** restricting a member's ability to assign their interest in the LLC.

The Articles of Organization must be signed by two or more individuals acting as organizers of the LLC.

Send the original and an exact copy of the Articles of Organization together with a check or money order in the amount of $250.00 payable to the State of Alaska to:

The State of Alaska
Division of Banking, Securities, and Corporations
P.O. Box 110808
Juneau, AK 99811-0808
Telephone (907) 465-2530

Alaska Form (continued)

Please do not write in this space (for Department use only)

ARTICLES OF ORGANIZATION
(Domestic Limited Liability Company)

The undersigned persons acting as organizers of a limited liability company under the Alaska Limited Liability Act (AS 10.50) hereby adopt the following Articles of organization:

Article I

The name of the limited liability company (LLC) is:

_____

Article II

The purpose for which the LLC is organized:

_____

S.I.C. codes: Primary _____   Secondary _____   Other _____

Article III

1. The name of the LLC's registered agent:

_____

2. The mailing address of the LLC's registered agent (if the mailing address is a P.O. Box, include a physical address):

_____

Article IV

If applicable, the latest date or event which will cause the LLC to cease to exist:

_____

_____

_____

08-430 (Rev. 6/95)

Alaska Form (continued)

Article V

1. The affairs of the LLC will be: (check one box)

   ❑ Managed by the members.   ❑ Managed by a manager.

2. If applicable, the name and address of the LLC's manager (optional):

   _____

3. If member managed, the names and address of the LLC's members (optional):

   _____

   _____

   _____

Attach list of additional names if necessary.

Article VI

If applicable, the terms and conditions restricting a member's ability to assign their interest in the LLC.

_____

_____

_____

_____

_____

_____

Attach additional pages if necessary.

Attach additional pages for including any other optional articles governing the regulation of the internal affairs of the LLC, consistent with this Act and the laws of this state.

Signed this _____ day of _____, 19 _____.

Name   Address

_____   _____

_____   _____

_____   _____

_____   _____

08-430 (Rev. 6/95)

Arizona Forms

STATE OF ARIZONA

OFFICE OF THE

CORPORATION COMMISSION

The following is a list of the mandatory information required in the Articles of Organization of an Arizona Limited Liability Company. (This is not intended for use as a blank form, but as a guideline only.) You may include any other provision in your Articles that is consistent with the Arizona Limited Liability Company Act (A.R.S. §29-601 et seq.)

ARTICLES OF ORGANIZATION

Pursuant to A.R.S. §29-632 the undersigned states as follows:

1. The name of the limited liability company is

   _____

2. The address of the registered office in Arizona is

   _____

   _____

   located in the County of_____

3. The statutory agent's name and address is_____

   _____

   _____

4. There are or will be two or more members at the time the limited liability company is formed.

5. The latest date on which the limited liability company is to

   dissolve is_____

   A. (Check appropriate Box.)

   [ ] Management of the limited liability company is vested in a manager or managers.

   [ ] Management of the limited liability company is reserved to the members.

Arizona Forms (continued)

B. (Check appropriate box.)

The name and address of each person who is a [ ] Manager [ ] Member at the time of formation of the limited liability company is:

_____

_____

_____

Signed: _____ Date _____

Signed: _____ Date _____

I, _____ having been designated to act as Statutory Agent, hereby consent to act in that capacity until removed or resignation is submitted in accordance with the Arizona Revised Statutes.

_____
(Signature of Statutory Agent)

Filing Fee: $50.00 (U.S.)
(Please make check payable to the Arizona Corporation Commission)

- 2 -

LL:04
REV/8/92   DOMESTIC

Arizona Forms (continued)

<u>NOTICE</u>
(for publication)

ARTICLES OF ORGANIZATION HAVE BEEN FILED IN THE OFFICE OF THE
ARIZONA CORPORATION COMMISSION FOR

I

Name: _____

II

The address of the registered office is: _____

_____

_____

The name and address of the Statutory Agent is: _____

_____

_____

III
(Please check A or B.)

[A]_____ Management of the Limited Liability Company is vested in
a Manager or Managers.

The name and address of each Manager at the time of formation of
the Limited Liability Company is:

_____

_____

_____

_____

[B]_____ Management of the Limited Liability Company is reserved
to the members.

The name and address of each member at the time of formation of the
Limited Liability Company is:

_____

_____

_____

_____

LL:01

Arkansas Form

Instructions: File in **DUPLICATE** with the Secretary of State
A copy will be returned after filing has been completed.
PLEASE TYPE OR CLEARLY PRINT IN INK

State of Arkansas - Office of Secretary of State
ARTICLES OF ORGANIZATION

The undersigned authorized manager or member or person forming this Limited Liability Company under the Small Business Entity Tax Pass Through Act, Act 1003 of 1993, adopt the following Articles of Organization of such Limited Liability Company:

First: The Name of the Limited Liability Company is:

_____

Must contain the words "Limited Liability Company," "Limited Company," or the abbreviation "L.L.C.," "L.C.," "LLC," or "LC." The word "Limited" may be abbreviated as "Ltd.", and the word "Company" may be abbreviated as "Co." Companies which perform PROFESSIONAL SERVICE MUST additionally contain the words "Professional Limited Liability Company," "Professional Limited Company," or the abbreviations "P.L.L.C.," "P.L.C.," "PLLC," or "PLC." The word "Limited" may be abbreviated as "Ltd." and the word "Company" may be abbreviated as "Co."

Second: Address of registered office of the Limited Liability Company which may be, but need not be, the place of business shall be:

_____

_____

_____

Third: The name of the registered agent and the business residence or mailing address of said agent shall be:

_____

_____

_____

(a) Acknowledgment and acceptance of appointment **MUST** be signed. I hereby acknowledge and accept the appointment of registered agent for and on behalf of the above named Limited Liability Company.

_____
Please sign here

Fourth: The latest date (month, day, year) upon which this Limited Liability Company is to dissolve:

_____

Fifth: IF THE MANAGEMENT OF THIS COMPANY IS VESTED IN A MANAGER OR MANAGERS, A STATEMENT TO THAT EFFECT MUST BE INCLUDED IN THE SPACE PROVIDED OR BY ATTACHMENT:

_____

PLEASE TYPE OR PRINT CLEARLY IN INK THE NAME OF THE PERSON (S) AUTHORIZED TO EXECUTE THIS DOCUMENT.

_____

Signature of authorized manager, member, or person forming this Company: _____
Filing Fee $50.00   LL-01

California Forms

State of California
Bill Jones
Secretary of State

LLC-12

LIMITED LIABILITY COMPANY
STATEMENT OF INFORMATION

IMPORTANT - Read the instructions before completing the form
This document is presented for filing pursuant to Section 17060 of the California Corporations Code.

| 1. Limited liability company name: | 2. File number: · |
| | 3. State/Country of Formation |

IF THERE HAS BEEN NO CHANGE IN ANY OF THE INFORMATION ON FILE--PROCEED TO LINE 10 (SEE INSTRUCTIONS)

4. Enter the name of the agent for service of process:

Name:

California street address if agent is an individual. (Do not use P.O. Box) Do not include address if agent is a corporation.
Address: City: State: **CALIFORNIA**   Zip Code:

5. Street address of the principal executive office:

Street address:

City: State: Zip Code:

6. In the case of a domestic limited liability company, the street address of the office required to be maintained pursuant to subdivision (a) of Section 17057:

Street address: City: State: **CALIFORNIA**   Zip Code:

7. Name , title and complete business or residential address of the manager(s) or, if none have been appointed or elected, of each member and executive officer, if any:

Name and title:	Name and title:
Address:	Address:
City: State: Zip Code:	City: State: Zip Code:

8. General type of business activity:

9. Number of pages attached, if any:

For Secretary of State Use

10. It is hereby declared that I am the person who executed this instrument, which execution is my act and deed.

Signature of authorized person

Type or print name and title - (Manager, Managing Member or Attorney-In-Fact)

Date: _____ , 19 _____

DUE DATE:

LLC-12   Approved by the Secretary of State

Filing Fee $10   1/96

California Forms (continued)

State of California
Bill Jones
Secretary of State

LLC-12

LIMITED LIABILITY COMPANY
STATEMENT OF INFORMATION

<u>IMPORTANT</u> - Read the instructions before completing the form
This document is presented for filing pursuant to Section 17060 of the California Corporations Code.

| 1. Limited liability company name: | 2. File number: |
| | 3. State/Country of Formation |

IF THERE HAS BEEN NO CHANGE IN ANY OF THE INFORMATION ON FILE–PROCEED TO LINE 10 (SEE INSTRUCTIONS)

4. Enter the name of the agent for service of process:

Name:

California street address if agent is an individual. (Do not use P.O. Box) Do not include address if agent is a corporation.

Address: City: State: **CALIFORNIA**   Zip Code:

5. Street address of the principal executive office:

Street address:

City: State: Zip Code:

6. In the case of a domestic limited liability company, the street address of the office required to be maintained pursuant to subdivision (a) of Section 17057:

Street address: City: State: **CALIFORNIA**   Zip Code:

7. Name , title and complete business or residential address of the manager(s) or, if none have been appointed or elected, of each member and executive officer, if any:

Name and title:	Name and title:
Address:	Address:
City: State: Zip Code:	City: State: Zip Code:

8. General type of business activity:

9. Number of pages attached, if any:

For Secretary of State Use

10. It is hereby declared that I am the person who executed this instrument, which execution is my act and deed.

_____
Signature of authorized person

_____
Type or print name and title - (Manager, Managing Member or Attorney-In-Fact)

Date: _____ , 19 _____

DUE DATE:

LLC-12   Approved by the Secretary of State

Filing Fee $10   1/96

California Forms (continued)

INSTRUCTIONS FOR COMPLETING THE STATEMENT OF INFORMATION (LLC-12)

All references are to the California Corporations Code unless otherwise indicated.
Type or legibly print in black ink.

DO NOT ALTER THE FORM

- Every limited liability company must file a statement of information within ninety (90) days of filing its original articles of organization or application for registration. Thereafter, every limited liability company must annually file a statement of information during the applicable filing period which is the calendar month during which its original articles of organization or application for registration was filed and the immediate preceding five months. The due date appears in the bottom left corner of the form. Section 17060.

- If the name of the agent for service of process or the street address of the individual designated as agent for service of process changes, the limited liability company must file a current statement of information. When any information required pursuant to subdivision (a) of Section 17060 changes the limited liability company must file a current statement of information. Section 17060(d).

Item 1. Enter the name of the limited liability company as registered with the Secretary of State of California. Section 17060(a)(1).

Item 2. Enter the file number issued by the Secretary of State of California. Section 17060(a)(1).

Item 3. Enter the jurisdiction of formation of the limited liability company. Section 17060(a)(1).

If there has been a change proceed to Item 4. If there has been no change, skip Items 4 through 9 and proceed to Item 10. If the filing is the initial statement of information complete the form in its entirety. Section 17060(b).

Item 4. Enter the name of the agent for service of process on the limited liability company.

If an individual is designated as the agent for service of process, enter a business or residential street address in California. Box number and "in care of" (c/o) are not acceptable. Do not enter an address if a corporation is designated as the agent for service of process and has filed a certificate pursuant to Section 1505 of the California Corporations Code. Section 17060(a)(2).

Item 5. Enter the street address of the principal executive office of the limited liability company which may be located either in California or in another jurisdiction. Section 17060(a)(4).

Item 6. If the limited liability company was organized under the laws of California, enter the street address of the office required to be maintained pursuant to subdivision (a) of Section 17057. Section 17060(a)(4).

Item 7. Enter the name, title, and business or residential address of any manager or managers, or if none have been elected or appointed, of each member and the executive officer, if any. Attach additional pages if necessary. Section 17060(a)(4).

Item 8. Briefly describe the general type of business that constitutes the principal business activity of the limited liability company. For example, manufacturer of aircraft, wholesale liquor distributor, or retail department store. Section 17060(a)(5).

Item 9. Enter the number of pages attached to the form, if any.

Item 10. The statement of information must be executed with an original signature. Facsimiles and photocopies of the statement of information are not acceptable for the purpose of filing with the Secretary of State.

- The fee for filing the statement of information with the Secretary of State is ten dollars ($10). Section 17701(k).

- Return the acknowledgment of filing to:

  Name:_____
  Firm/Company:_____
  Address:_____
  City:_____
  State:_____ Zip Code: _____

- Send the executed document and filing fee to:

  Office of the Secretary of State
  Limited Liability Company Unit
  P.O. Box 944228
  Sacramento, CA 94244-2280

LLC-12A

Colorado Form

Secretary of State
Corporations Section

For office use only	031

MUST BE TYPED
FILING FEE: $50.00
MUST SUBMIT TWO COPIES

Please include a typed
self-addressed envelope

ARTICLES OF ORGANIZATION

I/We the undersigned natural person(s) of the age of eighteen years or more, acting as organizer(s) of a limited liability company under the Colorado Limited Liability Company Act, adopt the following Articles of Organization for such limited liability company:

FIRST: The name of the limited liability company is: _____

SECOND: Principal place of business (if known): _____

_____

THIRD: The street address of the initial registered office of the limited liability company is: _____

_____

The mailing address (if different from above) of the initial registered office of the limited liability company is:

_____

The name of its proposed registered agent in Colorado at that address is: _____

_____

FOURTH: _____ The management is vested in managers (check if appropriate)

FIFTH: The names and business addresses of the initial manager or managers or if the management is vested in the members, rather than managers, the names and addresses of the member or members are:

NAME   **ADDRESS (include zip codes)**

_____   _____

_____   _____

SIXTH: The name and address of each organizer is:

NAME   **ADDRESS (include zip code)**

_____   _____

_____   _____

Signed_____   Signed_____
                                                                    Organizer
                                                                    Organizer

Revised 7/95

Connecticut Form

ARTICLES OF ORGANIZATION
DOMESTIC LIMITED LIABILITY COMPANY
LLC   Rev. 9/94

State of Connecticut
Secretary of the State

NOTE: This form constitutes only the minimum statutory requirements for filing with the Office of the Secretary of the State. Should you wish to include additional information, you may attach a plain sheet of 8½x11 paper to the document.

1. The name of the limited liability company:

_____

2. The nature of business to be transacted or the purpose to be promoted or carried out by the limited liability company is as follows:

3. Principal office address: (P.O. Box is <u>not</u> acceptable)_____

_____

4. Statutory agent for service of process, P.A. 93-267 §5:
    Name: Business Address:
                             _____
                             Residence Address: _____
                             _____

5. The latest date upon which the limited liability company will dissolve:
    _____

<u>EXECUTION</u>

6. Dated this_____day of_____, 19_____

7. _____   8. _____
    Name of Organizer (print or type)   Signature

9. Acceptance of appointed statutory agent.

    _____   10. _____
             Name (print or type)   Signature

For Official Use Only | Rec; CC:
                               | _____
                               | _____
                               | _____
                               | _____
                               | _____
                               | _____
                               |
                               Please provide filer's name and
                               complete address for mailing receipt

J150.4

Delaware Form

[SPECIMEN FORM NOT TO BE USED FOR FILING]

> **CAVEAT**: Counsel will note that the Delaware Limited Liability Company Act provides both for a *certificate of formation*, which is filed with the Delaware Secretary of State, and for a *limited liability company agreement*, which need not be filed with the Secretary of State. Inasmuch as a limited liability company agreement would apparently have to be drafted *ad hoc* for each limited liability company, it is recommended that Counsel examine the provisions of the Delaware Limited Liability Company Act prior to drafting both these documents. The annexed CSC brochure DELAWARE - LIMITED LIABILITY COMPANY - FORMATION is intended to assist Counsel in this research.

CERTIFICATE OF FORMATION

OF

_____

The undersigned, an authorized natural person, for the purpose of forming a limited liability company, under the provisions and subject to the requirements of the State of Delaware (particularly Chapter 18, Title 6 of the Delaware Code and the acts amendatory thereof and supplemental thereto, and known, identified, and referred to as the "Delaware Limited Liability Company Act"), hereby certifies that:

FIRST: The name of the limited liability company (hereinafter called the "limited liability company") is

SECOND: The address of the registered office and the name and the address of the registered agent of the limited liability company required to be maintained by Section 18-104 of the Delaware Limited Liability Company Act are Corporation Service Company, 1013 Centre Road, Wilmington, Delaware 19805.

Executed on   , 19   .

_____
[Typewritten name], Authorized Person

DE LL D-:CERTIFICATE OF FORMATION 06/96

District of Columbia Form

WRITTEN CONSENT TO ACT AS REGISTERED AGENT

TO: THE SUPERINTENDENT OF CORPORATIONS
      BUSINESS REGULATION ADMINISTRATION
      DEPT. OF CONSUMER & REGULATORY AFFAIRS
      WASHINGTON, DC

(A) BY A DISTRICT OF COLUMBIA RESIDENT

I, A BONAFIDE RESIDENT OF THE DIRECT OF
THE DISTRICT OF COLUMBIA HEREIN CONSENT TO ACT AS A REGISTERED
AGENT FOR:

ADDRESS OF REGISTERED AGENT:

Washington, DC

SIGNATURE OF REGISTERED AGENT: _____

DATE: _____

(B) BY A LEGALLY AUTHORIZED CORPORATION

THE CORPORATION HEREIN NAMED IS:

_____

AN AUTHORIZED CORPORATE REGISTERED AGENT IN THE DISTRICT OF
COLUMBIA, PER SIGNATURES OF IT'S PRESIDENT/VICE-PRESIDENT AND
SECRETARY/ASSISTANT SECRETARY, HEREIN CONSENTS TO ACT AS
REGISTERED AGENT FOR:

SIGNATURE: _____   OF PRESIDENT
           NAME: _____   OR VICE-PRESIDENT

  ATTEST: _____   OF SECRETARY
          NAME: _____   OR ASST. SECRETARY

DATE:

District of Columbia Form (continued)

ARTICLES OF ORGANIZATION

OF

_____

The undersigned being at least eighteen years of age, acting as the organizer of a limited liability company pursuant to Title 29 Chapter 13, of the Code of Laws of the District of Columbia, adopt the following Articles of Organization for such limited liability company:

FIRST: The name of the limited liability company is:

SECOND: The lastest date on which the limited liability company is to be dissolved is:

THIRD: The limited liability company is organized for any legal and lawful purpose pursuant to the District of Columbia Limited Liability Company Act. Also,

FOURTH: The address of the principal place of business is

and the name and business address of the agent for service of process is
Washington, DC .

FIFTH: The limited liability company shall be managed by managers and the names and business addresses of the initial managers are:

SIXTH: The name and address of the organizer is:

1013 Centre Road
Wilmington, DE 19805

Date: October 10, 1995   _____

Organizer

Florida Forms

ARTICLES OF ORGANIZATION FOR FLORIDA LIMITED LIABILITY COMPANY

ARTICLE I - Name:

The name of the Limited Liability Company is:

ARTICLE II - Address:

The mailing address and street address of the principal office of the Limited Liability Company is:

ARTICLE III - Duration:

The period of duration for the Limited Liability Company shall be:

ARTICLE IV - Management:
(check and complete the appropriate statement)

❏ The Limited Liability Company is to be managed by a manager or managers and the name(s) and address(es) of such manager(s) who is/are to serve as manager(s) is/are:

❏ The Limited Liability Company is to be managed by the members and the name(s) and address(es) of the managing member(s) is/ are:

ARTICLE V - Admission of Additional Members:

The right, if given, of the remaining members to admit additional members and the terms and conditions of the admissions shall be:

ARTICLE VI - Members Rights to Continue Business:

The right, if given, of the remaining members of the limited liability company to continue the business on the death, retirement, resignation, expulsion, bankruptcy, or dissolution of a member or the occurrence of any other event which terminates the continued membership of a member in the limited liability company shall be:

NOTE: If no provisions are to be made in Artice V and VI remove this page before submitting for filing with the Department of State.

Georgia Forms

THIS IS NOT A FORM - USE ONLY AS A GUIDE

**SAMPLE FORMAT
FOR
ARTICLES OF ORGANIZATION
(PLEASE TYPE)**

**ARTICLES OF ORGANIZATION OF
(EXACT NAME OF THE LIMITED LIABILITY COMPANY)**

I.

The name of the limited liability company is _____

_____.

(NOTE: PARAGRAPH II. BELOW IS OPTIONAL AND IS NOT REQUIRED BY LAW TO BE INCLUDED IN THE ARTICLES OF ORGANIZATION.)

II.

Management of the limited liability company is vested in one or more managers whose names and addresses are as follows:

_____

_____

_____.

This _____ day of _____, 199__.

Signed_____
ORGANIZER

_____
(PRINT NAME)

Georgia Forms (continued)

MAX CLELAND
Secretary of State
State of Georgia

BUSINESS INFORMATION AND SERVICES

J. K. JACKSON
Director

**TRANSMITTAL INFORMATION FOR GEORGIA
LIMITED LIABILITY COMPANIES**

DO NOT WRITE IN SHADED AREA - SOS USE ONLY

DOCKET # _____ PENDING CONTROL # _____ CONTROL # _____

Docket Code _____ LLC Type _____

Date Filed _____ Amount Received $ _____ Check/Receipt # _____

Jurisdiction (County) Code _____

Examiner _____ Date Completed _____

NOTICE TO APPLICANT: PRINT PLAINLY OR TYPE REMAINDER OF THIS FORM.
INSTRUCTIONS ARE ON THE BACK OF THIS FORM.

1. _____
   LLC Name Reservation Number

   _____
   LLC Name (exactly as appears on name reservation)

2. _____ _____
   Applicant/Attorney   Telephone Number

   _____
   Address   City   State   Zip Code

3. Name and Address of each organizer (attach additional sheets if necessary)

   _____
   Organizer   Address   City   State   Zip Code

   _____
   Organizer   Address   City   State   Zip Code

4. _____
   Name of Registered Agent in Georgia

   _____
   Registered Office Street Address in Georgia
                                              GA
   _____
   City   County   State   Zip Code

5. _____
   Principal Place of Business Mailing Address City   State   Zip Code

6. **NOTICE:** This form does not replace the articles of organization. Mail or deliver to the Secretary of State at the above address the following: (1) an original and one copy of this form; (2) an original and one copy of the articles of organization; and (3) a filing fee of $75.00 (make check payable to "Secretary of State").

   _____   _____
   Authorized Signature   Date
   (Member, Manager, or Organizer)

BR231 (06-95)

Georgia Forms (continued)

INSTRUCTIONS FOR COMPLETING BSR FORM BR231 (3/94)

THIS FORM MUST BE FILED WITH ALL NEW GEORGIA LIMITED LIABILITY COMPANIES. INFORMATION CONTAINED ON THIS FORM WILL BE ENTERED INTO THE SECRETARY OF STATE BUSINESS REGISTRATION DATABASE. THE FORM MUST BE TYPED OR PRINTED IN ENGLISH AND MUST BE DARK ENOUGH TO BE PHOTOCOPIED, MICROFILMED, OR OTHERWISE REPRODUCED. THIS FORM DOES NOT REPLACE THE ARTICLES OF ORGANIZATION. ALL INFORMATION ON THIS FORM MUST BE COMPLETED AND THE FORM FILED WITH THE ARTICLES OF ORGANIZATION OR THE ARTICLES WILL BE REJECTED FOR FILING.

1. LIMITED LIABILITY COMPANY NAME/NAME RESERVATION NUMBER (THIS INFORMATION IS REQUIRED.) List the exact limited liability company name and the name reservation number printed on the name reservation certificate.

2. APPLICANT/ATTORNEY. List the name and address of the applicant or filing attorney. The certificate of organization and any further correspondence regarding the filing will be mailed to this address.

3. NAME AND ADDRESS OF EACH ORGANIZER. List the name and address of each organizer of the limited liability company. Attach additional sheets if necessary.

4. REGISTERED AGENT/REGISTERED OFFICE. List the name of the registered agent (AGENT MUST BE IN GEORGIA). List the exact business address and county of the registered office. (THE BUSINESS ADDRESS MUST BE A STREET ADDRESS, NOT A POST OFFICE BOX, AND MUST BE IN GEORGIA.)

5. PRINCIPAL PLACE OF BUSINESS MAILING ADDRESS. List the mailing address of the limited liability company's principal place of business.

6. SIGNATURE. This form must be signed by a member, manager, or organizer.

BR231 (09-93)

Hawaii Form

DEPARTMENT OF COMMERCE AND CONSUMER AFFAIRS
Business Registration Division
1010 Richards Street
Mailing Address: P. O. Box 40, Honolulu, HI 96810

INSTRUCTIONS FOR PREPARING AND FILING ARTICLES OF ORGANIZATION
Hawaii Uniform Limited Liability Company Act
(Section 203, Hawaii Revised Statutes)

1.   Articles of Organization must be typewritten or printed in BLACK INK, and must be legible. All signatures must be in BLACK INK.

2.   One original executed document must be filed with the division, together with the filing fee. If you want stamped copies, submit the number of copies you want stamped, which will be returned to you after the articles have been processed.

3.   Certified Copies. <u>This is optional.</u> If you want certified copies, submit the number of copies you want certified, together with the original articles and fees. Fee for one certified copy is $10 plus 25¢ per page.

4.   Check that all information has been entered on the form, and that all typing or printing is legible.

5.   Fees must be submitted with the document. Make checks payable to the DEPARTMENT OF COMMERCE AND CONSUMER AFFAIRS, for the exact amount. Filing fees are not refundable. There is a $15.00 fee plus interest charge on all dishonored checks.

6.   Date of registration will be the date the Articles of Organization is filed in compliance with the Uniform Limited Liability Company Act.

Article I: State the exact company name. The name must contain the words "Limited Liability Company", or the abbreviation "L.L.C." or "LLC".

Article II: State the street address of the company's initial designated office in Hawaii. If no specific street address is available, state the rural route post office number or post office box designated by the United States Postal Service.

Article III: State the name and street address of the company's agent for service of process.

Article IV: State the name and street address of each organizer of the company.

Article V: Check whether the period of duration of the company is at-will or for a specified term. Enter the expiration date if duration is for a specified term.

Article VI: Check whether the company is manager-managed or member-managed, and state the names and residence street addresses of either the initial managers if manager-managed or the initial members if member-managed.

Article VII: Check whether the members are liable or not liable for the debts, obligations and liabilities of the company.

Execution: The form must be signed and certified by each organizer of the company. Signature must be in BLACK INK.

4/97
LLC

Hawaii Form (continued)

Nonrefundable Filing Fee: $100
Submit Original and One True Copy

DOMESTIC LLC

STATE OF HAWAII
DEPARTMENT OF COMMERCE AND CONSUMER AFFAIRS
Business Registration Division
1010 Richards Street
Mailing Address: P. O. Box 40, Honolulu, HI 96810

ARTICLES OF ORGANIZATION

(Section 428-203, Hawaii Revised Statutes)

PLEASE TYPE OR PRINT LEGIBLY IN BLACK INK

The undersigned, for the purpose of forming a limited liability company under the laws of the State of Hawaii, do hereby make and execute these Articles of Organization:

I

The name of the company shall be:

_____

Note: *The name must contain the words "Limited Liability Company" or the abbreviation "L.L.C." or "LLC".*

II

The street address of the initial designated office in Hawaii is:

_____

III

The company shall have and continuously maintain in the State of Hawaii an agent and street address of the agent for service of process on the company. (The agent must be an individual resident of Hawaii, a domestic corporation, or another domestic limited liability company.)

a.   The name of the company's initial agent for service of process is:

_____

b.   The street address of the agent for service of process is:

_____

LLC-3
4/97

1

L13 (Fee)
S21 (SH)

Hawaii Form (continued)

IV

The name and address of each organizer is:

_____   _____

_____   _____

_____   _____

_____   _____

_____   _____

V

The period of duration is: (*check one*)

[ ]   at-will

[ ]   for a specified term to expire on _____
                                                (Month, day, year)

VI

The company is: (*check one*)

[ ]   manager-managed, and the names and residence street addresses of the initial managers are listed below.

[ ]   member-managed, and the names and residence street addresses of the initial members are listed below.

_____   _____

_____   _____

_____   _____

_____   _____

VII

The members of the company:

[ ]   shall not be liable for the debts, obligations and liabilities of the company.

[ ]   shall be liable for some or all, as stated below, of the specified debts, obligations and liabilities of the company, and have consented in writing to the adoption of this provision or to be bound by this provision.

_____

_____

_____

2

Hawaii Form (continued)

VIII

(Optional provisions for the regulation of the internal affairs of the company as may be appropriate. If none, leave blank.)

We certify, under the penalties set forth in the Hawaii Uniform Limited Liability Company Act, that we have read the above statements and that the same are true and correct.

Signed this _____ day of _____, 19_____.

_____
(Type/Print Name of Organizer)

_____
(Type/Print Name of Organizer)

_____
(Signature of Organizer)

_____
(Signature of Organizer)

3

Idaho Forms

ARTICLES OF ORGANIZATION
LIMITED LIABILITY COMPANY

To the Secretary of State of Idaho,
Statehouse, Boise, Idaho 83720

1. The name of the limited liability company is: _____

_____

2. The address of the initial registered office is: _____
   (not a PO Box)

_____ and the name of the initial registered

agent at that address is: _____

Signature of registered agent : _____

3. The latest date certain on which the limited liability company will dissolve:_____

4. Is management of the limited liability company vested in a manager or managers?
   ☐ Yes   ☐ No   (check appropriate box)

5. If management is vested in one or more manager(s), list the name(s) and address(es) of at
   least one initial manager. If management is vested in the members, list the name(s) and
   address(es) of at least one initial member.

   Name: **Address:**

   _____   _____

   _____   _____

   _____   _____

   _____   _____

6. Signature of at least one person listed in #5 above:

   _____

   _____

   _____   _____
                                     Secretary of State use only
   _____

   _____

Idaho Forms (continued)

ARTICLES OF ORGANIZATION
PROFESSIONAL LIMITED LIABILITY COMPANY

To the Secretary of State of Idaho,
Statehouse, Boise, Idaho 83720

1. The name of the professional limited liability company is: _____

_____

2. The professional limited liability company is organized for the practice of the profession(s) of: _____

_____

3. The address of the initial registered office is _____
   (not a PO Box)

_____ , and the name of the

   initial registered agent at that address is _____

   Signature of registered agent: _____

4. The latest date certain on which the professional limited liability company will dissolve is:

_____

5. Is management of the limited liability company vested in a manager or managers?
   ☐ Yes   ☐ No   (check appropriate box)

6. If management is vested in one or more manager(s), list the name(s) and address(es) of at least one initial manager. If management is vested in the members, list the name(s) and address(es) of at least one member.

   <u>Name:</u>   <u>Address:</u>

   _____   _____

   _____   _____

   _____   _____

   _____   _____

   _____   _____

7. Signature(s) of at least one person listed in #6 above:

   _____

   _____

   _____

   _____

	Secretary of State use only

LLC3/593   File Two Copies   Fee: $100 if typed with no attachments
                                                 $120 if not typed or if attachments are included

Illinois Form

Form LLC-5.5
January 1994

George H. Ryan
Secretary of State
Department of Business Services
Limited Liability Company Division
Room 357, Howlett Building
Springfield, IL 62756

Payment must be made by certified
check, cashier's check, Illinois attorney's
check, Illinois C.P.A.'s check or money
order, payable to "Secretary of State."

Illinois
Limited Liability Company Act
Articles of Organization

Filing Fee $500.
SUBMIT IN DUPLICATE
Must be typewritten

This space for use by Secretary of State

Date
Assigned File #
Filing Fee $
Approved:

This space for use by
Secretary of State

1.   Limited Liability Company Name: _____

(The LLC name must contain the words limited liability company or L.L.C. and cannot contain the terms corporation, corp., incorporated, inc., ltd., co., limited partnership, or L.P.)

2.   Transacting business under an assumed name   ☐ Yes   ☐ No.
If YES, a Form LLC-1.20 is required to be completed and attached to these Articles.)

3.   The address, including county, of its principal place of business. (Post office box alone and c/o are unacceptable.) _____

4.   Federal Employer Identification Number (F.E.I.N.): _____

5.   The Articles of Organization are effective on: (Check one)

a)_____ the filing date, or b) _____ another date later than but not more than 60 days subsequent to the filing date: _____
(month, day, year)

6.   The registered agent's name and registered office address is:

Registered agent:

| First Name | Middle initial | Last name |

Registered Office:
(P.O. Box alone and
c/o are unacceptable)

| Number | Street | Suite # |
| City | Zip Code | County |

7.   Purpose or purposes for which the LLC is organized: Include the business code # (Form 1065)
(If not sufficient space to cover this point, add one or more sheets of this size.)

8.   The latest date the company is to dissolve _____.
(month, day, year)

And other events of dissolution enumerated on an attachment.

Illinois Form (continued)

LLC-5.5

9. Other provisions for the regulation of the internal affairs of the LLC per Section 5-5 (a) (8) included as attachment

☐ Yes ☐ No

10. a) Management is vested, in whole or in part, in managers ☐ Yes ☐ No
List their names and business addresses

b) Management is retained, in whole or in part, by the members ☐ Yes ☐ No
List their names and addresses

11. Name(s) & Address(es) of Organizer(s)

The undersigned affirms, under penalties of perjury, having authority to sign hereto, that this articles of organization is to the best of my knowledge and belief, true, correct and complete.

Dated _____ 19 ____

Signature and Name   **Business Address**

1. _____
Signature
_____
(Type or print name and title)
_____
(Name if a corporation or other entity)

1. _____
Number   *Street*
_____
City/Town
_____
State   *Zip Code*

2. _____
Signature
_____
(Type or print name and title)
_____
(Name if a corporation or other entity)

2. _____
Number   *Street*
_____
City/Town
_____
State   *Zip Code*

3. _____
Signature
_____
(Type or print name and title)
_____
(Name if a corporation or other entity)

3. _____
Number   *Street*
_____
City/Town
_____
State   *Zip Code*

(Signatures must be in ink on an original document. Carbon copy, photocopy or rubber stamp signatures may only be used on conformed copies.)

C-281

Indiana Form

[SPECIMEN FORM NOT TO BE USED FOR FILING]

CAVEAT: Counsel will note that the Indiana Business Flexibility Act, the basic statute governing limited liability companies in that state, provides both for *articles of organization*, which are filed with the Indiana Secretary of State, and for an *operating agreement*, which need not be filed with the Secretary of State. Inasmuch as an operating agreement would apparently have to be drafted *ad hoc* for each limited liability company, it is recommended that Counsel examine the provisions of the Indiana Business Flexibility Act prior to drafting both these documents. Special provisions apply to limited liability companies with professional service purposes.

ARTICLES OF ORGANIZATION

OF

_____

The undersigned person, acting as an organizer of the limited liability company hereinafter named, sets forth the following statements.

FIRST: The name of the limited liability company (the "company") is

SECOND: The street address of the company's registered office in the State of Indiana and the name of the company's registered agent at that address are

[Adapt or take one of the following for Article THIRD]

THIRD: The latest date on which the company is to dissolve is

, 19

THIRD: The duration of the company is perpetual until dissolution in accordance with the provisions of the Indiana Business Flexibility Act.

[Adapt or take the following, if applicable, for Article FOURTH]

FOURTH: The management of the business and affairs of the company is vested in a manager or managers.

Executed on: , 19   .

_____
, Organizer

IN LL D-:ARTICLES OF ORGANIZATION 01/96

Iowa Form

[Submit 1 originally executed (or facsimile) copy]

[SPECIMEN FORM NOT TO BE USED FOR FILING]

> **CAVEAT**: Counsel will note that the Iowa Limited Liability Company Act provides both for *articles of organization*, which is filed with the Iowa Secretary of State, and for an *operating agreement*, which need not be filed with the Secretary of State. Inasmuch as an operating agreement would apparently have to be drafted *ad hoc* for each limited liability company, it is recommended that Counsel examine the provisions of the Iowa Limited Liability Company Act prior to drafting both these documents.

ARTICLES OF ORGANIZATION

OF

_____

FIRST: The name for the limited liability company (the "company") is

SECOND: The street address of the company's initial registered office and the name of the company's initial registered agent at that office are Corporation Service Company, 729 Insurance Exchange Building, Des Moines, Iowa 50309.

THIRD: The street address of the company's principal office within or without the State of Iowa is

FOURTH: The duration of the company shall expire on

19

Executed on   , 19   .

_____
                                                                  Organizer

IA LL D-:ARTICLES OF ORGANIZATION 07/96

Kansas Form

[Submit 1 original signed copy
and 1 signed or conformed copy]

[SPECIMEN FORM NOT TO BE USED FOR FILING]

> **CAVEAT**: Counsel will note that the Kansas Limited Liability Company Act provides both for *articles of organization*, which is filed with the Kansas Secretary of State, and for an *operating agreement*, which need not be filed with the Secretary of State. Inasmuch as an operating agreement would apparently have to be drafted *ad hoc* for each limited liability company, it is recommended that Counsel examine the provisions of the Kansas Limited Liability Company Act prior to drafting both these documents.

ARTICLES OF ORGANIZATION

OF

_____

FIRST: The name of the limited liability company (the "company") is

SECOND: The latest date on which the company is to dissolve is

THIRD: The purpose for which the company is organized is

FOURTH: The address of the company's registered office in the State of Kansas is c/o Corporation Service Company, Suite 1108, 534 South Kansas Avenue, Topeka, Kansas 66603, and the name and the address of the company's initial resident agent in the State of Kansas are Corporation Service Company, Suite 1108, 534 South Kansas Avenue, Topeka, Kansas 66603.

KS LL D-:ARTICLES OF ORGANIZATION 03/96-1

Kansas Form (continued)

[Take or adapt one of the following for Article FIFTH]

FIFTH: The members of the company have the right to admit additional members to the company. The terms and conditions of the admission of additional members to the company are

FIFTH: The members of the company do not have the right to admit additional members to the company, except as the provisions of Section 17-7618 may otherwise permit.

[Adapt the following for Article SIXTH]

SIXTH: The remaining members of the company [do not] have the right to continue the business of the company on the death, retirement, resignation, expulsion, bankruptcy, or dissolution of a member or on the occurrence of any other event which terminates the continued membership of a member in the company.

[Adapt one of the following for Article SEVENTH]

SEVENTH: The company is to be managed by a manager or managers. The name and the address of each such manager who is to serve as a manager of the company until his or her successor is elected and qualifies are:

NAME   ADDRESS

SEVENTH: The management of the company is reserved to the members of the company. The names and the addresses of the members of the company are:

NAME   ADDRESS

[Here set forth other desired provisions, if any. KLLCA 17-7607]

KS LL D-:ARTICLES OF ORGANIZATION 03/96-2

Kansas Form (continued)

IN WITNESS WHEREOF, we have hereunto set our hands this   day of
, 19   .

_____
                                                                                 Member

_____
                                                                                 Member

KS LL D-:ARTICLES OF ORGANIZATION 03/96-3

Kentucky Form

ARTICLES OF ORGANIZATION

OF

A LIMITED LIABILITY COMPANY

FIRST: The name of the limited liability company is:

SECOND: The Company shall exist for a period of thirty (30) years from and after the date the Kentucky Secretary of State issues Articles of Organization, unless dissolved earlier by law.

THIRD: The principal mailing address of the limited liability company is

FOURTH: The company's registered office in the State of Kentucky is to be located at 828 Lane Allen Road, #F-4, Lexington, KY, 40504, and its registered agent at such address is Corporation Service Company d/b/a CSC-Lawyers Incorporating Service Company.

FIFTH: The company will be managed by the managers/members and the street addresses of those who are to serve until the first meeting of managers/members or until their successors are elected are:

NAME   ADDRESS

SIXTH. The will be no less than two members.

SEVENTH. The name and address of the organizer is:

NAME   ADDRESS

IN WITNESS WHEREOF, the undersigned, being the individual forming the Company, has executed, signed and acknowledged the Articles of Organization this   of   ,   .

_____
                    Organizer

Louisiana Form

[Must be filed with official form Limited Liability Company Initial Report]

[SPECIMEN FORM NOT TO BE USED FOR FILING]

> **CAVEAT**: Counsel will note that the Limited Liability Company Law of Louisiana provides both for *articles of organization*, which are filed with the Louisiana Secretary of State, and for an *operating agreement*, which need not be filed with the Secretary of State. Inasmuch as an operating agreement would apparently have to be drafted *ad hoc* for each limited liability company, it is recommended that Counsel examine the provisions of the Limited Liability Company Law prior to drafting both these documents. The annexed CSC brochure LOUISIANA - LIMITED LIABILITY COMPANY - FORMATION is intended to assist Counsel in this research.

ARTICLES OF ORGANIZATION

OF

(Under Section 12:1305 of the Limited Liability Company Law of the State of Louisiana)

FIRST: The name of the limited liability company (the "company") is

[Take or adapt 1 of the following for Article SECOND]

SECOND: The purposes for which the company is formed are

[here insert specific purposes]

SECOND: The purpose of the company is to engage in any lawful activity for which limited liability companies may be formed under the provisions of the Limited Liability Company Law of the State of Louisiana.

LA LL D-:ARTICLES OF ORGANIZATION 10/96-1 (LALLCART)

Louisiana Form (continued)

[The remaining provisions are optional]

[Take, adapt, or omit 1 of the following for Article THIRD]

THIRD: The limitations on the authority of the members to bind the company are contained in a written operating agreement.

THIRD: The limitations on the authority of members to bind the company are as follows:

[here insert limitations]

THIRD: There are no limitations on the authority of members to bind the company.

[Take, adapt, or omit 1 of the following for Article FOURTH]

FOURTH: The company will not be managed by mangers.

FOURTH: The company will be managed by mangers to the following extent:

[here set forth desired provisions]

[Take, adapt, or omit 1 of the following for Article FIFTH]

FIFTH: The restrictions on the authority of managers are as follows:

[here insert desired provisions]

FIFTH: The restrictions on the authority of managers are contained in a written operating agreement.

[Take, adapt, or omit 1 of the following for Article SIXTH]

SIXTH: The latest date on which the company is to dissolve is

, 19

LA LL D-:ARTICLES OF ORGANIZATION 10/96-2 (LALLCART)

Louisiana Form (continued)

SIXTH: The latest date on which the company is to dissolve is not to be set forth herein.

[The articles of organization may contain "a statement that persons dealing with the limited liability company may rely upon a certificate of one or more managers, members, or other certifying officials, whose names are included in the statement, to establish the membership of any member, the authenticity of any records of the limited liability company, or the authority of any person to act on behalf of the limited liability company, including but not limited to the authority to take the actions referred to in R.S. 12:1318(B), unless otherwise provided in the articles of organization".]

Signed on   , 19   .

_____
, Organizer

STATE OF   )
) SS.:
COUNTY OF   )

On this   day of   , 19   , before me, the subscriber, a Notary Public duly appointed to take proof and acknowledgment of deeds and other instruments, came   , to me personally known to be the individual described in and who signed the preceding articles of organization, and who duly acknowledged to me, the signing of the same, and being by me duly sworn deposeth and saith that he signed the foregoing articles of organization as organizer.

IN TESTIMONY WHEREOF, I hereunto set my hand and affix my official seal at   ,   the day and year first above written.

_____
Notary Public

(SEAL)

LA LL D-:ARTICLES OF ORGANIZATION 10/96-3 (LALLCART)

Maine Form

CAVEAT: Counsel will note that the Massachusetts Limited Liability Company Act provides both for *a certificate of organization*, which is filed with the State Secretary, and for an *operating agreement*, which need not be filed with the State Secretary. Inasmuch as an operating agreement would apparently have to be drafted *ad hoc* for each limited liability company, it is recommended that Counsel examine the provisions of the Massachusetts Limited Liability Company Act prior to drafting both these documents.

[File 1 executed original]

CERTIFICATE OF ORGANIZATION

OF

(Pursuant to the provisions of Section 12 of the
Massachusetts Limited Liability Company Act)

To the State Secretary
Commonwealth of Massachusetts

It is hereby certified that:

FIRST: The name of the limited liability company (the "company") is

SECOND: The address of the office of the company in the Commonwealth of Massachusetts, required to be maintained by the provisions of Section 5 of the Massachusetts Limited Liability Company Act, and where the records are to be kept as prescribed by the provisions of Section 9 of said Act, is:

MA LL D:-CERTIFICATE OF ORGANIZATION 01/96-1

Maine Form (continued)

ORGANIZER(S)*   DATED _____

_____   _____
          (signature)   (type or print name)

_____   _____
          (signature)   (type or print name)

_____   _____
          (signature)   (type or print name)

For Organizer(s) which are Entities

Name of Entity _____

By _____   _____
          (authorized signature)   (type or print name and capacity)

Name of Entity _____

By _____   _____
          (authorized signature)   (type or print name and capacity)

Name of Entity _____

By _____   _____
          (authorized signature)   (type or print name and capacity)

THE FOLLOWING SHALL BE COMPLETED BY THE REGISTERED AGENT *UNLESS* THIS DOCUMENT IS ACCOMPANIED BY FORM MLLC-18 (§607.2.).

The undersigned hereby accepts the appointment as registered agent for the above named limited liability company.

REGISTERED AGENT   DATED _____

_____   _____
          (signature)   (type or print name)

For Registered Agent which is a Corporation

Name of Corporation _____

By _____   _____
          (authorized signature)   (type or print name and capacity)

*Articles must be signed by all organizers (§627.1.A.). The execution of the articles constitutes an oath or affirmation, under the penalties of false swearing under Title 17-A, section 453, that, to the best of the signers' knowledge and belief, the facts stated in the articles are true (§627.3.).

SUBMIT COMPLETED FORMS TO: SECRETARY OF STATE, STATION #101, AUGUSTA, ME 04333-0101
ATTN: CORPORATE EXAMINING SECTION
TEL. (207) 287-4195

FORM NO. MLLC-6   95

Maryland Form

[SPECIMEN FORM NOT TO BE USED FOR FILING]

CAVEAT: Counsel will note that the Maryland Limited Liability Company Act provides both for *articles of organization*, which is filed with the Maryland State Department of Assessments and Taxation, and for an *operating agreement*, which need not be filed with the Department. Inasmuch as an operating agreement would apparently have to be drafted *ad hoc* for each limited liability company, it is recommended that Counsel examine the provisions of the Maryland Limited Liability Company Act prior to drafting both these documents. The annexed CSC brochure MARYLAND - LIMITED LIABILITY COMPANY - FORMATION is intended to assist Counsel in this research.

ARTICLES OF ORGANIZATION

OF

_____

FIRST: The name of the limited liability company (the "company") is

SECOND: The latest date on which the company is to dissolve is

THIRD: The purpose for which the company is formed is

FOURTH: The address of the company's principal office in the State of Maryland is: c/o CSC-Lawyers Incorporating Service Company, 11 East Chase Street, Baltimore, Maryland 21202, and the name and the address of the company's resident agent in the State of Maryland are CSC-Lawyers Incorporating Service Company, 11 East Chase Street, Baltimore, Maryland 21202.

IN WITNESS WHEREOF, I have adopted and signed these articles of organization and do hereby acknowledge that the adoption and signing are my act.

Dated:

_____
, Authorized Person

MD LL D-:CERTIFICATE OF FORMATION 03/96

Massachusetts Form

[SPECIMEN FORM NOT TO BE USED FOR FILING]

CAVEAT: Counsel will note that the Massachusetts Limited Liability Company Act provides both for *a certificate of organization*, which is filed with the State Secretary, and for an *operating agreement*, which need not be filed with the State Secretary.   Inasmuch as an operating agreement would apparently have to be drafted *ad hoc* for each limited liability company, it is recommended that Counsel examine the provisions of the Massachusetts Limited Liability Company Act prior to drafting both these documents.

[File 1 executed original]

CERTIFICATE OF ORGANIZATION

OF

(Pursuant to the provisions of Section 12 of the
Massachusetts Limited Liability Company Act)

To the State Secretary
Commonwealth of Massachusetts

It is hereby certified that:

FIRST: The name of the limited liability company (the "company") is

SECOND: The address of the office of the company in the Commonwealth of Massachusetts, required to be maintained by the provisions of Section 5 of the Massachusetts Limited Liability Company Act, and where the records are to be kept as prescribed by the provisions of Section 9 of said Act, is:

MA LL D:-CERTIFICATE OF ORGANIZATION 01/96-1

Massachusetts Form (continued)

THIRD: The name and the address within the Commonwealth of Massachusetts of the resident agent for service of process for the company is:

[Take or adapt one of the following for Article FOURTH]

FOURTH: The latest date on which the company is to dissolve is

, 19   .

FOURTH: The company is not to have a specific date of dissolution.

[Take or adapt one of the following for Article FIFTH]

FIFTH: The name and the address of each manager of the company at the time of its formation are:

NAME   ADDRESS

FIFTH: The company does not have managers at the time of its formation.

SIXTH: The general character of the company's business is as follows:

[If the LLC is not to have managers, at least one person must be
named in the following Article. If the LLC is to have managers
this Article is optional. MLLCA 12]

_____: The name of each person who is authorized to execute any documents
to be filed with the Office of the State Secretary is

[The certificate of organization may "set forth...any other matters
the authorized persons determine to be included therein". The
following Article is optional.]

MA LL D:-CERTIFICATE OF ORGANIZATION 01/96-2

Massachusetts Form (continued)

_____: The name of each person authorized to execute, acknowledge, deliver, and record any recordable instrument purporting to affect an interest in real property, whether to be recorded with a Registry of Deeds or with a District Office of the Land Court is:

IN WITNESS WHEREOF AND UNDER THE PENALTIES OF PERJURY, the person whose signature appears below does hereby affirm and execute this certificate of organization as an authorized person this   day of   , 19   .

_____
Authorized Person

MA LL D:-CERTIFICATE OF ORGANIZATION 01/96-3

Michigan Forms

C&S 700 (Rev. (5/95)

MICHIGAN DEPARTMENT OF COMMERCE - CORPORATION AND SECURITIES BUREAU	
Date Received	(FOR BUREAU USE ONLY)

Name

Address

City	State	Zip Code

EFFECTIVE DATE:

☞ **Document will be returned to the name and address you enter above** ☜

ARTICLES OF ORGANIZATION
For use by Domestic Limited Liability Companies
(Please read information and instructions on last page)

B ☐ ☐ ☐ ☐ ☐ ☐

Pursuant to the provisions of Act 23, Public Acts of 1993, the undersigned execute the following Articles:

ARTICLE I

The name of the limited liability company is: _____

ARTICLE II

The purpose or purposes for which the limited liability company is formed is to engage in any activity within the purposes for which a limited liability company may be formed under the Limited Liability Company Act of Michigan.

ARTICLE III

The duration of the limited liability company is: _____

ARTICLE IV

1. The address of the registered office is:

_____ , Michigan _____
(Street Address)   (City)   (ZIP Code)

2. The mailing address of the registered office if different than above:

_____ , Michigan _____
(P.O. Box)   (City)   (ZIP Code)

3. The name of the resident agent at the registered office is: _____

ARTICLE V (Insert any desired additional provision authorized by the Act; attach additional pages if needed.)

Signed this _____ day of _____ , 19_____

By _____   _____   _____
(Signature)   (Signature)   (Signature)

_____   _____   _____
(Type or Print Name)   (Type or Print Name)   (Type or Print Name)

Michigan Forms (continued)

C&S 700

Name of Person or Organization Remitting Fees:

_____

Preparer's Name and Business Telephone Number:

_____

(   ) _____

INFORMATION AND INSTRUCTIONS

1. The articles of organization cannot be filed until this form, or a comparable document, is submitted.

2. Submit one original of this document. Upon filing, the document will be added to the records of the Cor   :ion and Securities Bureau. The original will be returned to the address you enter in the box on the front as evidence of filing.

   Since this document will be maintained on optical disc media, it is important that the filing be legible. Documents with poor black and white contrast, or otherwise illegible, will be rejected.

3. This document is to be used pursuant to the provisions of Act 23, P.A. of 1993, by two or more persons for the purpose of forming a domestic limited liability company. **Use form 701 if the Limited Liability Company will be providing a personal service for which a license or legal authorization is required pursuant to Article 9 of the Act.**

4. Article I - The name of a domestic limited liability company is required to contain one of the following words or abbreviations: "Limited Liability Company", "L.L.C.", or "L.C."

5. Article II - Under section 203(b) of the Act, it is sufficient to state substantially, alone or with specifically enumerated purposes, that the limited liability company is formed to engage in any activity within the purposes for which a limited liability company may be formed under the Ac'

6. Article III - The term of existence of the limited liability company must be reflected as a specific date, a number of years, or perpetual.

7. Article IV - A post office box may not be designated as the address of the registered office.

8. This document is effective on the date endorsed "Filed" by the Bureau. A later effective date, no more than 90 days after the date of delivery, may be stated as an additional article.

9. The articles must be signed in ink by two or more of the persons who will be members. Names of person signing shall be stated beneath their signatures.

10. If more space is needed, attach additional pages. All pages should be numbered.

11. FEES: Make remittance payable to the State of Michigan. Include limited liability company name on check or money order. **Nonrefundable filing fee** **$50.00**

Michigan Forms (continued)

MICHIGAN DEPARTMENT OF COMMERCE - CORPORATION AND SECURITIES BUREAU	
Date Received	(FOR BUREAU USE ONLY)

Name

Address

City   State   Zip Code

EFFECTIVE DATE.

☜ Document will be returned to the name and address you enter above ☞

L C — ☐ ☐ ☐

ARTICLES OF ORGANIZATION
For use by Domestic Professional Service Limited Liability Companies

(Please read information and instructions on last page)

Pursuant to the provisions of Act 23, Public Acts of 1993, the undersigned execute the following Articles:

ARTICLE I

The name of the professional limited liability company is:

ARTICLE II

The limited liability company is organized for the sole and specific purpose of rendering the following professional service(s):

ARTICLE III

The duration of the limited liability company is:_____

ARTICLE IV

1. The address of the registered office is:

_____ , Michigan _____
   (Street Address)   (City)   (ZIP Code)

2. The mailing address of the registered office if different than above:

_____ , Michigan _____
   (P O Box)   (City)   (ZIP Code)

3. The name of the resident agent at the registered office is: _____

Michigan Forms (continued)

ARTICLE V

All members will be duly licensed or otherwise legally authorized to render one or more of the professional service(s) for which this limited liability company is organized except as otherwise provided in Section 904(2) of this Act or prohibited by law.

Signed this _____ day of _____, 19_____

_____   _____
(Signature)   (Signature)

_____   _____
(Type or Print Name)   (Type or Print Name)

_____   _____
(Signature)   (Signature)

_____   _____
(Type or Print Name)   (Type or Print Name)

Minnesota Form

STATE OF MINNESOTA
ARTICLES OF ORGANIZATION FOR
A LIMITED LIABILITY COMPANY
MINNESOTA STATUTES CHAPTER 322B

FOR OFFICE USE ONLY
Filing date: _____
Charter # _____ LLC
Page # _____

PLEASE TYPE OR PRINT IN BLACK INK.

<u>Before Completing this Form Please Read the Instructions on the Back.</u>   FILING FEE $135.00

1. Name of Company: _____

2. Registered Office Address:

_____ MN _____
Complete Street Address or Rural Route and Rural Route Box Number   City   State   ZIP Code
        (P.O. Box is Unacceptable)

3. Name of Registered Agent (optional): _____

4. Business Mailing Address: (if different from registered office address)

_____
          Address   City   State   ZIP Code

5. Desired Duration of LLC: (in years - 30 year limit) _____

    list your SIC Code. _____ Select one of the 2-digit SIC codes listed on the reverse side of this form that most accurately describes the nature of the business you are forming.

7. The members of this company (check one)   do ___ do not ___ have the power to avoid dissolution by giving dissolution avoidance consent in the case of occurrence of events listed in section 322B.801, subdivision 1, clause (5).

8. The members of this company (check one)   do___ do not ___ have the power to enter into a business continuation agreement.

9. Does this LLC own, lease or have any interest in agricultural land or land capable of being farmed?
    (Check One)   Yes ___   No ___

10. Name and Telephone Number of Contact Person for this LLC:

    Name_____ Phone (___) _____

11. Name and Address of Organizer(s):

Name (print)	Complete Address	Original Signature (required)

Mississippi Form

OFFICE OF THE MISSISSIPPI SECRETARY OF STATE
P. O. BOX 136, JACKSON, MS 39205   601-359-1333

Instructions For Forming A
Mississippi Limited Liability Company

1. Enclose document with correct filing fee to Secretary of State.

2. The document must be filed with an exact or conformed copy.

3. Document must be typewritten or printed in black ink. Use only one side of a page.

4. Provide complete street address and mailing address where registered office is located.

5. The document must be executed in the name of the Limited Liability Company by (1) any manager, if management of the Limited Liability Company is vested in one or more managers, or by a member if management of the Limited Liability Company is reserved to the members; (2) if the Limited Liability Company has not been formed, by any person forming the Limited Liability Company or (3) if the Limited Liability Company is in the hands of a receiver, trustee or other court-appointed fiduciary, by that fiduciary.

6. Enclose a stamped, self addressed envelope for return mailing of evidenced copy of filing.

Fee Schedule

DOCUMENT	FORM NO.	FEE
Certificate of Formation	F100	$50
Certificate of Amendment	F101	$50
Certificate of Dissolution or Cancellation	F103	$25
Certificate of Merger	F102	$25
Certificate of Change of Address of Registered Agent	F122	$25

Mississippi Form (continued)

OFFICE OF THE MISSISSIPPI SECRETARY OF STATE
P. O. BOX 136, JACKSON, MS 39205   601-359-1333

Certificate of Formation
(Attach duplicate)

The undersigned, pursuant to Senate Bill No. 2395, Chapter 402, Laws of 1994, hereby executes the following Certificate of Formation and sets forth:

1. Name of the Limited Liability Company:

2. Federal Tax ID: ➡

3. Name, street and mailing address of the registered agent and office:

4. If the Limited Liability Company is to have a specific date of dissolution, the latest date upon which the Limited Liability Company is to dissolve:

5. Is full or partial management of the Limited Liability Company vested in a manager or managers? (Check appropriate box)   ☐ Yes   ☐ No

6. Other matters the managers or members elect to include:

Mississippi Form (continued)

By: (Printed Name/Title)

Signature:

Street and Mailing Address:

By: (Printed Name/Title)

Signature:

Street and Mailing Address:

Missouri Form

State of Missouri

Rebecca McDowell Cook, Secretary of State
P.O. Box 778, Jefferson City, Mo. 65102

Corporation Division

Articles of Organization
(Submit in duplicate with filing fee of $105)

1. The name of the limited liability company is:

   _____

2. The purpose(s) for which the limited liability company is organized: _____

   _____

   _____

3. The name and address of the limited liability company's registered agent in Missouri is:

   _____
   Name   Street address   City/State/Zip

4. The management of the limited liability company is vested in one or more managers.   ☐ Yes ☐ No

5. The latest date on which the limited liability company is to dissolve is: _____
                                                                              Month/Day/Year

6. Upon the withdrawal of any member, the remaining member(s) have the following right(s) (if any) to continue the business and affairs of the limited liability company:

   _____

7. The name(s) and address(es) of each organizer:

   _____

   _____

   _____

8. For tax purposes, is the limited liability company considered a corporation?   ☐ Yes   ☐ No

In affirmation thereof, the facts stated above are true:

_____ Organizer

_____ Organizer

_____ Organizer

LLC-1 (12-94)

Montana Form

STATE OF MONTANA

ARTICLES *of* ORGANIZATION *for*
DOMESTIC LIMITED LIABILITY COMPANY
(35-8-202, MCA)

Prepare, sign and submit an original and copy with fee.
This is the minimum information required.

(For use by the Secretary of State only)

MAIL TO: MIKE COONEY
Secretary of State
P.O. Box 202801
Helena, MT 59620-2801
☎(406)444-3665

Form: PLC-1
Filing Fee: $70.00

▶ *Executed by the undersigned for the purpose of forming a Montana Limited Liability Company.*

PLEASE CHECK ONE BOX:
☐Limited Liability Company   ☐Professional Limited Liability Company

▶ FIRST: The name of the limited liability company is (must contain "limited liability company", "limited company" or if Professional, "professional limited liability company", or an abbreviation)

_____

▶ SECOND: The name and address of its registered office/agent is:

Name _____

Address _____

_____, MONTANA Zip Code _____

▶ THIRD: The address of its principal place of business in Montana:

Address _____

City _____, MONTANA Zip Code _____

▶ FOURTH: The latest date on which the LLC is to dissolve is _____.

▶ FIFTH: The LLC will be managed by a ☐Manager *or* by its ☐Members.

▶ SIXTH: The names of the Managers or Members and street addresses are:

_____

_____

_____

▶ SEVENTH: *If a Professional Limited Liability Company*, the services to be provided

_____

_____
Dated

_____
Signature of Organizer

_____
Printed Name and Address

Nebraska Form

Secretary of State
1301 State Capitol
Lincoln, NE 68509
402/471-4079

ARTICLES OF ORGANIZATION
LIMITED LIABILITY COMPANY

1. The name of the limited liability company is:_____

_____

2. The period of duration is _____ years. (Not to exceed thirty years)

3. The purpose for which the limited liability company is organized: _____

_____

_____

_____

_____

4. The address of its principal place of business in Nebraska is:

_____
Street Address

_____ NE _____
City   Zip Code

The name and address of the registered agent in Nebraska is:

_____
Name of Registered Agent

_____
Street Address

_____ NE _____
City   Zip Code

5. The total amount of cash contributed to stated capital is $_____.

A description and agreed value of property other than cash contributed:

_____

_____

_____

6. The total additional contributions agreed to be made by all members and the times
at which or events upon the happening of which the contributions will be made:

_____

_____

_____

Nebraska Form (continued)

7. The right, <u>if given</u>, of the members to admit additional members and the terms and conditions of the admission.

    _____

    _____

    _____

8. The right, <u>if given</u>, of the remaining members to continue the business on the death, retirement, resignation, expulsion, bankruptcy, or dissolution of the member or on the occurrence of any other event which terminates the continued membership of a member.

    _____

    _____

    _____

9a. If the company is to be managed by a manager(s), list the name and address of the manager(s).

    _____

    _____

    _____

9b. If the management is reserved to the members, list the names and addresses of the members:

<u>Members Name</u>	<u>Address</u>
_____	_____
_____	_____
_____	_____
_____	_____
_____	_____
_____	_____
_____	_____
_____	_____

10. Any other provisions, not inconsistent with the law, which the members elect to set out in the articles of organization for the regulation of the internal affairs of the limited liability company.

    _____

    _____

FILING FEE: $100.00 plus $3.00 per page and $10.00 for a certificate

Nebraska Form (continued)

State of _____ }ss   _____
County of _____ }   Signature of Member

_____ being first duly sworn on oath deposes
and says that (he)(she) is the _____ of
_____ and that (he)(she) has signed the foregoing
document as _____ of the limited liability company and
the statements therein contained are true.
Subscribed and sworn to before me this_____day of_____19 _____.

  (notary seal)

                                        _____
                                        Signature of Notary

State of _____ }ss   _____
County of _____ }   Signature of Member

_____ being first duly sworn on oath deposes
and says that (he)(she) is the _____ of
_____ and that (he)(she) has signed the foregoing
document as _____ of the limited liability company and
the statements therein contained are true.
Subscribed and sworn to before me this_____day of_____19 _____.

  (notary seal)

                                          _____
                                        Signature of Notary

State of _____ }ss   _____
County of _____ }   Signature of Member

_____ being first duly sworn on oath deposes
and says that (he)(she) is the _____ of
_____ and that (he)(she) has signed the foregoing
document as _____ of the limited liability company and
the statements therein contained are true.
Subscribed and sworn to before me this_____day of_____19 _____.

  (notary seal)

                                          _____
                                        Signature of Notary

State of _____ }ss   _____
County of _____ }   Signature of Member

_____ being first duly sworn on oath deposes
and says that (he)(she) is the _____ of
_____ and that (he)(she) has signed the foregoing
document as _____ of the limited liability company and
the statements therein contained are true.
Subscribed and sworn to before me this_____day of_____19 _____.

  (notary seal)

                                          _____
                                        Signature of Notary

                    (may be photocopied)

Nevada Form

Articles of Organization
Limited-Liability Company
(PURSUANT TO NRS 86)
STATE OF NEVADA
Secretary of State

Filing fee: S125
Receipt #:

(For filing office use)   (For filing office use)

IMPORTANT: Read instructions on reverse side before completing this form.
TYPE OR PRINT (BLACK INK ONLY)

1. Name of Limited Liability Company: _____

2. Dissolution Date (latest date upon which the company is to dissolve): _____

3. Resident Agent: (designated resident agent and the <u>STREET ADDRESS</u> in Nevada where process may be served)

Name of Resident Agent: _____

Street Address: _____
                Street No.   **Street Name**   **City**   **Zip**

    Mailing Address (if different): _____

4. Right of remaining members of the company to continue the business on the death, retirement, resignation, expulsion, bankruptcy or dissolution of a member or occurrence of any other event which terminates the continued membership of a member in the company: _____ **YES** _____ **NO**

5. Management: The company shall be managed by _____ manager(s) **OR** _____ members
Names and addresses of manager(s) or members: (attach additional pages if necessary)
    1. _____
    2. _____

    If managed by members, members may contract debts on behalf of the company _____ **YES** _____ **NO**

6 .Other matters: This form includes the minimal statutory requirements to organize under NRS 86. Please attach any other information deemed appropriate. Number of pages attached _____.

7. Signature of organizer(s): The name(s) and address(es) of the organizer(s) executing the articles:
    <u>(Signatures must be notarized)</u> (Attach additional pages if there are more than two organizers)

_____   _____
Name (print)   **Name (print)**

_____   _____
Address   **City/State/Zip**   **Address**   **City/State/Zip**

_____   _____
Signature   **Date**   **Signature**   **Date**

8. Certificate of acceptance of appointment of resident agent:
I, _____ hereby accept appointment as resident agent
for the above named limited-liability company.
  By: _____   _____
Signature of resident agent   **Date**

Nevada Form (continued)

Articles of Organization
State of Nevada

INSTRUCTIONS
FOR FILING ARTICLES OF ORGANIZATION

1. Indicate the name of limited-liability company. The name must contain the words **LIMITED-LIABILITY COMPANY; LIMITED COMPANY or LIMITED** or the abbreviations L.L.C., L.C., LLC OR LC. The word "company" may also be abbreviated.

The name may not be the same as or deceptively similar to the name of a limited-liability company, limited partnership, limited-liability partnership, or corporation already on file in this office. A name may be reserved (if available) at the Office of the Secretary of State. For details or to check for availability you may call (702) 687-5203 or write to the Secretary of State, Capitol Complex, Carson City, NV., 89710.

2. State the latest date upon which the company is to dissolve.

3. Indicate the name and street address in Nevada of the resident agent for service of process. The resident agent must reside or be located in this state. The mailing address must be included if different from the physical address.

4. Indicate the right, if given, of the remaining members of the company to continue the business on the death, retirement, resignation, expulsion, bankruptcy, or dissolution of a member or occurrence of any other event which terminates the continued membership of a member in the company.

5. State any other provision, which the members elect to set out in the articles of organization for the regulation of the internal affairs of the company, including any provisions which under NRS Chapter 86 are required or permitted to be set out in the operating agreement of the company.

6. Limited-liability companies may be managed by either a manager(s) or by its members. If the management of a limited-liability company is reserved to the members, they must be listed and the rights stated, if any, of the members to contract debts on behalf of the company. The articles must list the names and addresses of one or more managers, or if there are no managers, two or more members. Please use letter size white paper to list additional managers or members.

7. One or more persons may organize a limited-liability company. Indicate the names and addresses of the organizer(s) executing the articles. Remember that organizer's signatures <u>must</u> be acknowledged.

8. Resident agent needs to sign certificate of acceptance to serve as agent for the limited liability company.

IMPORTANT

Copies: You must send in the number of copies you would like certified and returned to you in addition to the original articles to be filed. NRS 86.241 requires that a certified copy of the articles be kept in the records office of the company.

Fees: $125 filing fee and $10.00 for each certification.

Filing may be made at the Office of the Secretary of State in the State Capitol building or by mail to:

Secretary of State
Limited-Liability Company Division
Capitol Complex
Carson City, Nevada 89710
(702) 687-5203

(10/95)

New Hampshire Form

STATE OF NEW HAMPSHIRE

Fee for Form LLC 1A: $50.00
Filing fee: $35.00
Total fees $85.00
Use black print or type.
Leave 1" margins both sides.

Form No. LLC 1
RSA 304-C:12

CERTIFICATE OF FORMATION

THE UNDERSIGNED, UNDER THE NEW HAMPSHIRE LIMITED LIABILITY COMPANY LAWS
SUBMITS THE FOLLOWING CERTIFICATE OF FORMATION:

FIRST: The name of the Limited Liability Company is _____

_____

SECOND: The nature of the primary business or purposes are

_____

_____

_____

_____

THIRD: The name of the limited liability company's registered agent is

_____

and the street address (including zip code and post office box, if any) of its
registered office is (agent's business address) _____

_____

FOURTH: The securities (generally, membership interests) will be sold
or offered for sale within the meaning of RSA 421-B. (New Hampshire
Securities Act).

FIFTH: The latest date on which the limited liability company is to
dissolve is _____.

SIXTH: The management of the limited liability company _____ vested
in a manager or managers.

Dated _____, 19____

        Signature: _____

        Print or Type Name: _____

        Title: _____

New Jersey Form

New Jersey Department of State
Division of Commercial Recording
Certificate of Formation, Limited Liability Company

L-100 NJSA 42 (2/94)

This form may be used to record the formation of a Limited Liability Company under and by virtue of New Jersey State law. Applicants must insure strict compliance with NJSA 42, the New Jersey Limited Liability Company Act, and insure that all applicable filing requirements are met. This form is intended to simplify filing with the Secretary of State. Applicants are advised to seek out private legal assistance before submitting filings to the Secretary's office.

1. Name of Limited Liability Company:

2. The purpose for which this Limited Liability Company is organized is:

3. Date of formation:

4. Registered Agent Name & Address (must be in NJ):

5. Dissolution date:

6. Other provisions (list below or attach to certificate):

The undersigned represent(s) that this Limited Liability Company has two or more members, and that this filing complies with requirements detailed in NJSA 42. The undersigned hereby attest(s) that they are authorized to sign this certificate on behalf of the Limited Liability Company.

Name	Date

New Jersey Form (continued)

Instructions: Type all information except **signatures**.
Form must be completed and filed in duplicate.
The original document will be retained by the Division of Commercial Recording.

Remittance: Check or Money Order should be signed and made payable to the
Secretary of State, and be submitted with the document to be filed.
Filing Fee: $100.00   * Expedited Fee: $10.00 additional

* Expedited Service requests must be delivered in person or by messenger service such as Federal Express, Emery, UPS, or any overnight service, **but not** U.S. Postal Service Overnight because it does not directly deliver to our division office.

** Please use zip code **08625** for regular mail. Regular mail wrongly addressed to the "Expedited Service" zip code **08628** will be returned "undeliverable" by the local Post Office.

Certificate of Formation, Limited Liability Company
Title 42 New Jersey Business Corporation Act

1.   **NAME OF LIMITED LIABILITY COMPANY:**   LLC name must include the words "Limited Liability Company" or the abbreviation "L.L.C.".

2.   **PURPOSE:**   This is an optional field.

3.   **DATE OF FORMATION:**   May be left blank. If this field is left blank, the date of formation will be the date on which the Certificate of Formation is filed in the Office of the Secretary of State.

4.   **REGISTERED AGENT AND ADDRESS:**   May be an individual resident of this State whose business office is identical with the LLC's registered office, or a domestic or foreign authorized corporation having a business address identical with the LLC's registered office. Office must be located in this State.

5.   **DISSOLUTION DATE:**   If desired, enter the specific date of dissolution in this field.

THE PURPOSE OF THIS FORM IS TO SIMPLIFY THE FILING REQUIREMENTS OF THE SECRETARY OF STATE AND DOES NOT REPLACE THE NEED FOR COMPETENT LEGAL ADVICE.

New Mexico Form

```
FEE:  $50.00
Submit original and
one copy
Must be Typewritten
```

ARTICLES OF ORGANIZATION

OF

_____

(NAME OF LIMITED LIABILITY COMPANY)

The undersigned, acting as organizer(s) of a limited liability
company pursuant to the New Mexico Limited Liability Company Act,
adopt the following Articles of Organization:

ARTICLE 1 NAME

The name of the limited liability company is _____

_____.

ARTICLE 2 DURATION

The latest date upon which the Company is to dissolve is:_____

_____.

ARTICLE 3 AGENT AND ADDRESS

The street address and city of the Company's initial
registered office and the name of its initial registered agent at
that office is:_____

_____, and
the street address and city of the Company's principal place of
business, if different from its registered office, is _____

_____.

New Mexico Form (continued)

AFFIDAVIT OF ACCEPTANCE OF APPOINTMENT
BY DESIGNATED INITIAL REGISTERED AGENT

To the State Corporation Commission
State of New Mexico

STATE OF _____)
)
                                             S.S.:
)
COUNTY OF _____)

        The undersigned hereby accepts appointment as registered agent

for _____, a
limited liability company, which is named in the annexed Articles
of Organization.

                    _____
                    Registered Agent's Signature (Individual)

            OR

                    _____
                    Registered Agent's Name (Corporation, LCC)

        By _____
                    Signature of Agent's authorized
                    Representative

Subscribed and sworn to before me on _____

by_____ to me known to be the person
described   in   and   who executed the foregoing instrument and
acknowledged that he/she executed the same as his/her free act and
deed.

_____
    NOTARY PUBLIC

MY COMMISSION EXPIRES: _____

    (NOTARY SEAL)

New York Form

[NOTE: All documents to be filed by the Bureau of Corporations of the Department of State must be typed and signed in black. The Bureau of Corporations has construed General Construction Law Section 46 as authorizing conformed or facsimile signatures. A document which has been telecopied twice is NOT of acceptable quality for filing.]

[SPECIMEN FORM NOT TO BE USED FOR FILING]

CAVEAT: Counsel will note that the New York Limited Liability Company Law provides both for *articles of organization*, which are filed with the New York Department of State, and for an *operating agreement*, which need not be filed with the Department of State. Inasmuch as an operating agreement would apparently have to be drafted *ad hoc* for each limited liability company, it is recommended that Counsel examine the provisions of the New York Limited Liability Company Law prior to drafting both these documents.

<u>ARTICLES OF ORGANIZATION</u>

OF

_____

(Under Section Two Hundred Three of the Limited Liability Company Law)

The undersigned person, acting as an organizer of the limited liability company hereinafter named, sets forth the following statements.

<u>FIRST</u>: The name of the limited liability company (the "company") is

<u>SECOND</u>: The county within the State of New York in which the office of the company is to be located is the County of

[Adapt or take one of the following for Article THIRD]

<u>THIRD</u>: The latest date on which the company is to dissolve is
, 19   .

<u>THIRD</u>: The company is not to have a specific date of dissolution in addition to the events of dissolution set forth in Section 701 of the New York Limited Liability Company Law.

NY LL D-:ARTICLES OF ORGANIZATION 03/95-1

New York Form (continued)

FOURTH: The Secretary of State of the State of New York is designated as agent of the company upon whom process against it may be served. The post office address within or without the State of New York to which the Secretary of State of the State of New York shall mail a copy of any process against the company served upon him or her is c/o

[Adapt one of the following for Article FIFTH]

FIFTH: The company is to be managed by one or more members.

FIFTH: The company is to be managed by a class or classes of members.

FIFTH: The company is to be managed by one or more managers.

FIFTH: The company is to be managed by a class or classes or managers.

[The remaining optional provisions may be adapted if desired]

SIXTH: The name and the address within the State of New York of the registered agent of the company are:
The registered agent is to be the agent of the company upon whom process against it may be served.

SEVENTH: [All members of the company] [The members of the company hereinafter specified] are to be liable in their capacity as members for [all debts, obligations, or liabilities] [the debts, obligations, or liabilities hereinafter specified] of the company as authorized pursuant to Section 609 of the New York Limited Liability Company Law.

EIGHTH: The business purpose for which the company is formed is as follows:

NINTH: There are [no] limitations on the authority of [members] [managers] of the company to bind the company.

[If a delayed effective date, not more than 60 days after the date of the filing of articles of organization with the Department of State, is desired, adapt the following

_____: The company shall be formed on   , 19   .

NY LL D-:ARTICLES OF ORGANIZATION 03/95-2

New York Form (continued)

IN WITNESS WHEREOF, I have signed this document on the date set forth below and do hereby affirm, under penalties of perjury, that the statements contained therein have been examined by me and are true and correct. [In lieu of being signed and affirmed under penalties of perjury, the document may be signed and verified. See form of verification, infra.]

Dated: , 19

_____, Organizer

NY LL D-:ARTICLES OF ORGANIZATION 03/95-3

New York Form (continued)

Verification of Signer of Articles of Organization

STATE OF   )
) SS.:
COUNTY OF   )

                , being duly sworn, deposes and says that he is the person who signed the foregoing articles of organization; that he signed the said articles in the capacity set opposite or beneath his signature thereon; that he has read the said articles and knows the contents thereof; and that the statements contained therein are true to his own knowledge.

_____
               , Organizer

Subscribed and sworn to before me
on   , 19

_____
   Notary Public

NY LL D-:ARTICLES OF ORGANIZATION 03/95-4

New York Form (continued)

[Notice for Publication.   Adapt the following as applicable]

NOTICE CONTAINING SUBSTANCE OF ARTICLES OF ORGANIZATION

Name of limited liability company (LLC):

Date of filing articles of organization with secretary of state: , 19

County in which office of LLC is to be located:

The secretary of state has been designated as agent of the LLC upon whom process against it may be served. The post office address to which the secretary of state shall mail a copy of any process against it served upon him or her is:

Purpose of business of LLC:

Latest date upon which LLC is to dissolve is   , 19

Name and address of the registered agent of LLC, who is to be the agent of LLC against whom process against it may be served:

NY LL D-:ARTICLES OF ORGANIZATION - NOTICE 10/94

North Carolina Form

State of North Carolina
Department of the Secretary of State
LIMITED LIABILITY COMPANY
ARTICLES OF ORGANIZATION

Pursuant to §57C-2-20 of the General Statutes of North Carolina, the undersigned does hereby submit these Articles of Organization for the purpose of forming a limited liability company.

1. The name of the limited liability company is: _____

2. The latest date on which the limited liability company is to dissolve is: _____

3. The name and address of each organizer executing these articles of organization is as follows (at least two persons must execute this document; attach additional pages if necessary):

4. The street address and county of the initial registered office of the limited liability company is:

Number and Street _____

City, State, Zip Code _____   County _____

5. The mailing address **if different from the street address** of the initial registered office is: _____

_____

6. The named of the initial registered agent is: _____

7. Check one of the following:

_____ (i) Member-managed LLC: all of the members by virtue of their status as members shall be managers of this limited liability company.

_____ (ii) Manager-managed LLC: except as provided by N.C.G.S. §57C-3-20(a), the members of this limited liability company shall not be managers by virtue of their status as members.

8. Any other provisions which the limited liability company elects to include are attached.

9. These articles will be effective upon filing, unless a date and/or time is specified: _____

This the _____ day of _____ , 19_____

_____   _____
Signature   Signature

_____   _____
Type or Print Name and Title   Type or Print Name and Title

NOTES:
1. Filing fee is $100. This document and one exact or conformed copy of these articles must be filed with the Secretary of State.

North Carolina Forms (continued)

Instructions for Filing
LIMITED LIABILITY COMPANY
ARTICLES OF ORGANIZATION

Item 1	Enter the complete company name, which must include a limited liability company ending required by N.C.G.S. §57C-2-30(a) (limited liability company, L.L.C., LLC, ltd. liability co., limited liability co., or ltd. liability company).
Item 2	Enter the **latest** date on which the limited liability company may dissolve. See N.C.G.S. §57C-6-01.
Item 3	Enter the name and address of each organizer who executes the articles of organization.
Item 4	Enter the complete street address of the registered office and the county in which it is located.
Item 5	Enter the complete mailing address of the registered office **only** if mail is not delivered to the street address shown in Item 4 or if the registered agent prefers to have mail delivered to a P.O. Box or Drawer.
Item 6	Enter the name of the registered agent. The registered agent must be either an individual who resides in North Carolina; a domestic business corporation, nonprofit corporation, or limited liability company; or a foreign business corporation, nonprofit corporation, or limited liability company authorized to transact business in North Carolina.
Item 7	Unless the articles of organization provide otherwise, all members by virtue of their status as members shall be managers of the LLC, together with any other persons designated as managers in the LLC's written operating agreement. If the articles of organization provide that all members are not necessarily managers by virtue of their status as members, then those persons designated as managers in the operating agreement shall manage the LLC, except for such period during which no such designation has been made or is in effect, in which case all members shall be managers.
Item 8	N.C.G.S. §57C-2-21(b) states that the articles of organization may contain any provision not inconsistent with law, including any matter that under Chapter 57C is permitted to be set forth in a limited liability company's operating agreement.
Item 9	The document will be effective on the date and at the time of filing, unless a delayed date or an effective time (on the day of filing) is specified. If a delayed effective date is specified without a time, the document will be effective at 11:59 p.m. Raleigh, North Carolina time on the day specified. If a delayed effective date is specified with a time, the document will be effective on the day and at the time specified. A delayed effective date may be specified up to and including the 90th day after the day of filing.

Date and Execution

Enter the date the document was executed.

In the blanks provided enter:

- The name of the entities executing the Articles of Organization; if individuals, leave blank.
- The signatures of the organizers or representatives of the organizing entities.
- The names of the organizers or names and titles of the above-signed representatives.

This document may, but need not, contain an acknowledgement, verification, or proof.

ATTENTION: Limited liability companies wishing to render a professional service as defined in N.C.G.S. §55B-2(6) shall contact the appropriate North Carolina licensing board to determine whether compliance with additional licensing requirements may be mandated by law. Such limited liability companies should consult N.C.G.S. §57C-2-01 for further details.

North Dakota Form

SAMPLE FORMAT
ARTICLES OF ORGANIZATION OF
LIMITED LIABILITY COMPANY

(The **Bold** items are to be completed by the applicant)

I(We), the undersigned individual(s) of the age of eighteen years or more, acting as organizer(s) of a limited liability company organized under the North Dakota (**Limited Liability Company** or **Limited Liability Company Farming**) Act, adopt the following Articles of Organization for such limited liability company.

ARTICLE I: The name of the limited liability company is

ARTICLE II: The address of the principal executive office is
   The telephone number at that address is

ARTICLE III: The name of the registered agent is   whose social security number is
      The address of such agent is   This address shall be
the registered office in North Dakota.

ARTICLE IV: The names and addresses of the organizers are:

ARTICLE V: The period of duration is   from the date of filing of these Articles of Organization with the North Dakota Secretary of State, unless the limited liability company is sooner dissolved.

ARTICLE VI: The members **have (do not have)** the right to continue the limited liability company upon the occurrence of any event under N.D.C.C., subdivision e of Section 10-32-109 that terminates the continued membership of a member. The remaining members **will (will not)** have the power to avoid dissolution by giving dissolution avoidance consent.

ARTICLE VII: The members **have (do not have)** the power to enter into a business continuation agreement.

   I(We), the above named organizer(s) have read the foregoing Articles of Organization, know the contents, and believe the statements made therein to be true.

Dated: _____, 19____

_____   _____   _____

Ohio Form

Prescribed by
Bob Taft, Secretary of State

Approved _____
Date_____
Fee $85.00

Form LCA (July 1994)

ARTICLES OF ORGANIZATION

(Under Section 1705.04 of the Ohio Revised Code)
Limited Liability Company

The undersigned, desiring to form a limited liability company, under Chapter 1705 of the Ohio Revised Code, do hereby state the following:

FIRST: The name of said limited liability company shall be _____

_____

(the name must include the words "limited liability company", "limited", "Ltd" or "Ltd.")

SECOND: This limited liability company shall exist for a period of _____

_____

THIRD: The address to which interested persons may direct requests for copies of any operating agreement and any bylaws of this limited liability company is:

_____
(street or post office box)

_____
(city, village or township)   (state)   (zip code)

[ ]   Please check this box if additional provisions are attached hereto

Provisions attached hereto are incorporated herein and made a part of these articles of organization.

Ohio Form (continued)

FOURTH: Purpose (optional)

IN WITNESS WHEREOF, we have hereunto subscribed our names, this _____day of _____, 19_____ .

Signed:_____   Signed:_____

Signed:_____   Signed:_____

Signed:_____   Signed:_____

(If insufficient space for all signatures, please attach a separate sheet containing additional signatures)

INSTRUCTIONS

1.   The fee for filing Articles of Organization for a limited liability company is $85.00.

2.   Articles **will be returned unless** accompanied by a written appointment of agent signed by all or a majority of the members of the limited liability company which must include a written acceptance of the appointment by the named agent.

3.   A limited liability company must be formed by a minimum of two persons.

4.   Any other provisions that are from the operating agreement or that are not inconsistent with applicable Ohio law and that the members elect to set out in the articles for the regulation of the affairs of the limited liability company may be attached.

[Ohio Revised Code Section 1705.04]

Oklahoma Form

FEE: $100.00

ARTICLES
OF
ORGANIZATION

FOR OFFICE USE ONLY

PLEASE PRINT CLEARLY

FILE IN DUPLICATE

TO: THE OKLAHOMA SECRETARY OF STATE, 101 State Capitol, Oklahoma City, OK 73105

The undersigned, for the purpose of forming an Oklahoma limited liability company pursuant to the provisions of 18 O.S. 1992 Supp., Section 2004, does hereby execute the following articles:

1.   The name of the limited liability company (Note: The name must contain either the words "limited liability company" or the abbreviation "L.L.C." or the abbreviation "L.C."):

_____

_____

2.   The street address of its principal place of business in this state:

_____

Street address   City   State   Zip Code

3.   The name and address of the resident agent in the state of Oklahoma:

_____

Name   Street Address   City   State   Zip Code
                       (P.O. Boxes are not acceptable.)

4.   The latest date on which the limited liability company is to dissolve: _____

5.   The purposes for which the limited liability company is formed are:

Oklahoma Form (continued)

Articles of organization **must** be signed by at least one person who need not be a member of the limited liability company.

Dated: _____

_____
Signature

_____
Type or Print Name
(List title, if applicable)

_____
Address

(SOS FORM 0073-8/92)

Oregon Form

Submit the original
and one true copy
$40.00

Registry Number:

_____

Corporation Division - Business Registry
Public Service Building
255 Capitol Street NE, Suite 151
Salem, OR 97310-1327
(503) 986-2200 Facsimile (503) 378-4381

THIS SPACE FOR OFFICE USE ONLY

ARTICLES OF ORGANIZATION
Limited Liability Company
PLEASE TYPE OR PRINT LEGIBLY IN BLACK INK

ARTICLE 1: Name of the company: _____

Note: The name must contain the words "Limited Liability Company" or the abbreviation "L.L.C."

SIC Code: _____ (see back of this form)

ARTICLE 2: ☐ Latest date upon which the Limited Liabilty Company is to dissolve is_____
(Check one)   OR
☐ Duration shall be perpetual.

ARTICLE 3: Name of the initial registered agent: _____

Address of initial registered office (must be a street address in Oregon.)

_____ Oregon _____
Street and number   City   Zip code

ARTICLE 4: Address where the Division may mail notices if
different than registered agent's address: Attn:_____

_____
Street and number or PO box   City   State   Zip code

ARTICLE 5: Name and address of each organizer:

_____   _____

_____   _____

ARTICLE 6: Check the following statement if applicable:

☐   This limited liability company will be managed by a manager(s).

ARTICLE 7: Optional provisions: (attach a separate sheet if necessary)

Execution: _____ Organizer
Signature   Printed name   Title

_____ Organizer
Signature   Printed name   Title

Person to contact about this filing: _____
                                        Name   Daytime phone number
MAKE CHECKS PAYABLE TO THE CORPORATION DIVISION OR INCLUDE YOUR *VISA OR MASTERCARD* NUMBER AND
EXPIRATION DATE _____._____._____._____   ____/____ . SUBMIT THE COMPLETED FORM AND FEE TO
THE ABOVE ADDRESS OR FAX TO (503) 378-4381.

Pennsylvania Form

DSCB:15-8913 (Rev 95)-3

Department of State
Corporation Bureau
P. O. Box 8722
Harrisburg, PA 17105-8722

Instructions for Completion of Form:

A. One original of this form is required. The form shall be completed in black or blue-black ink in order to permit reproduction. The filing fee for this form is $100 made payable to the Department of State. PLEASE NOTE: A separate check is required for each form submitted.

B. Under 15 Pa.C.S. § 135(c) (relating to addresses) an actual street or rural route box number must be used as an address, and the Department of State is required to refuse to receive or file any document that sets forth only a post office box address.

C. The following, in addition to the filing fee, shall accompany this form:

    (1) Three copies of a completed form DSCB:15-134A (Docketing Statement).

    (2) Any necessary copies of form DSCB:17.2 (Consent to Appropriation of Name) or form DSCB:17.3 (Consent to Use of Similar Name).

    (3) Any necessary governmental approvals.

D. This form and all accompanying documents shall be mailed to:

Department of State
Corporation Bureau
P. O. Box 8722
Harrisburg, PA 17105-8722

E. To receive confirmation of the file date prior to receiving the microfilmed original, send either a self-addressed, stamped postcard with the filing information noted or a self-addressed, stamped envelope with a copy of the filing document.

Pennsylvania Form (continued)

Microfilm Number_____

Filed with the Department of State on_____

Entity Number_____

_____
Secretary of the Commonwealth

CERTIFICATE OF ORGANIZATION-DOMESTIC LIMITED LIABILITY COMPANY
DSCB:15-8913 (Rev 95)

In compliance with the requirements of 15 Pa.C.S. § 8913 (relating to certificate of organization), the undersigned, desiring to organize a limited liability company, hereby state(s) that:

1. The name of the limited liability company is: _____

2. The (a) address of this limited liability company's initial registered office in this Commonwealth or (b) name of its commercial registered office provider and the county of venue is:

(a) _____
Number and Street   City   State   Zip   County

(b) c/o: _____
Name of Commercial Registered Office Provider   County

For a limited liability company represented by a commercial registered office provider, the county in (b) shall be deemed the county in which the limited liability company is located for venue and official publication purposes.

3. The name and address, including street and number, if any, of each organizer are:

NAME   ADDRESS

_____

_____

_____

4. (Strike out if inapplicable): A member's interest in the company is to be evidenced by a certificate of membership interest.

5. (Strike out if inapplicable): Management of the company is vested in a manager or managers.

6. The specified effective date, if any is: _____
month   day   year   hour, if any

7. (Strike out if inapplicable): The company is a restricted professional company organized to render the following restricted professional service(s):

_____

_____

8. For additional provisions of the certificate, if any, attach an 8 1/2 x 11 sheet.

Pennsylvania Form (continued)

_CB:15-8913 (Rev 95)-2

IN TESTIMONY WHEREOF, the organizer(s) has (have) signed this Certificate of Organization this _____ day of _____ , 19 _____ .

_____
(Signature)

_____
(Signature)

_____
(Signature)

Rhode Island Form

§ RI:230 *Form:* Articles of organization

Filing Fee $150.00   LLC I.D. #...................................

State of Rhode Island and Providence Plantations
OFFICE OF THE SECRETARY OF STATE

CORPORATIONS DIVISION
100 NORTH MAIN STREET
PROVIDENCE, RI 02903

LIMITED LIABILITY COMPANY

ARTICLES OF ORGANIZATION

Pursuant to the provisions of Chapter 7-16 of the General Laws, 1956, as amended, the following Articles of Organization are adopted for the limited liability company to be organized hereby:

FIRST. The name of the Limited Liability company is:
....

SECOND. There are at least two members who have agreed to form this limited liability company.

THIRD. The latest date on which the limited liability company is to dissolve is:
....

FOURTH. The name and address of the resident agent in the State of Rhode Island is: ....
....
....
....

....
Signature of Registered Agent

FIFTH. Under the terms of these Articles of Organization and any written operating agreement made or intended to be made, the limited liability company is intended to be treated for purposes of federal income taxation as:

☐ a partnership;

or ☐ a corporation.

Rhode Island Form (continued)

SIXTH. Additional provisions (if any) not inconsistent with law, which the members elect to have set forth in these Articles of Organization:

SEVENTH. Date these Articles of Organization are to become effective, if later than the date of filing, is: .... (not more than 30 days after the filing of these Articles of Organization)

Dated ...., 19...........

....
(Signature of Authorized Person)

South Carolina Form

STATE OF SOUTH CAROLINA
SECRETARY OF STATE
JIM MILES
ARTICLES OF ORGANIZATION
FOR A
LIMITED LIABILITY COMPANY
WHICH SHALL RENDER PROFESSIONAL SERVICES

1. The name of the limited liability company which complies with § 33-43-103 of the 1976 South Carolina Code as amended is _____

    _____

2. The limited liability company's purpose shall be to render the following professional services in accordance with § 33-43-1104 of the 1976 South Carolina Code as amended

    _____

    _____The limited
    liability company may render services ancillary to the professional services, may invest its funds in real estate, mortgages, securities, or any other type of investment, but may not engage in other business activities except as may be specifically authorized by the licensing authorities of this State.

3. The street address of the initial registered office of the limited liability company is

    _____

                                                    Street Address

    _____
            City   County   Zip Code
    and the initial registered agent of the limited liability company at that office is

    _____

4. The latest date upon which the limited liability company is to dissolve _____

    _____

5. [ ]   Check this box only if management of the limited liability company is vested in a manager or managers.

    If this limited liability company is managed by managers, all of the managers shall be individuals who are authorized by law in this or another state to render a professional service which is rendered by this limited liability company.

6. This limited liability company may only admit as members individuals who are licensed by law in this or another state to render a professional service the limited liability company practices, and other entities as members only as permitted by § 33-43-801(C) of the 1976 South Carolina Code as amended.

South Carolina Form (continued)

7.   Set forth any other provisions which the organizers determine to include, including any provisions that are required or are permitted to be set forth in the limited liability company operating agreement: _____

_____
_____
_____
_____

8.   The following are the names and signatures of each person who is forming this limited liability company and who will be initial members. (Two persons who are licensed to render a professional service this limited liability company practices are required to form the limited liability company.)

_____   _____
Name   Signature

_____   _____
Name   Signature

_____   _____
Name   Signature

Date:_____

FILING INSTRUCTIONS

1.   File two copies of this form, the original and either a duplicate original or a conformed copy.

2.   If space on this form is not sufficient, please attach additional sheets containing a reference to the appropriate paragraph in this form, or prepare this using a computer disk which will allow for expansion of the space on the form.

3.   This form must be accompanied by the filing fee of $110.00 payable to the Secretary of State.

Form Approved by South Carolina
Secretary of State Jim Miles, June 1994

South Dakota Forms

Secretary of State
State of South Dakota
500 E. Capitol
Pierre, SD 57501-5070
605-773-4845

ARTICLES OF ORGANIZATION
DOMESTIC LIMITED LIABILITY COMPANY

1. The name of the limited liability company is _____ _____

   _____

2. The period of duration is _____ years.

3. The purpose for which the limited liability company is organized; _____

   _____

   _____

   _____

   _____

4. The address of its principal place of business in South Dakota is _____

   _____

5. The name of the registered agent is _____

   The address of the registered agent is _____

   _____

6. The total amount of cash is $ _____, and a description and agreed value of property
   or services initially or to be initially contributed:

   _____

   _____

   _____

   _____

7. The total additional contributions, if any, agreed to be made by all members and the times at which
   or events upon the happening of which they shall be made:

   _____

   _____

   _____

   _____

8. The right, if given, of the members to admit additional members, and the terms and conditions of
   the adminssion:

   _____

   _____

   _____

   _____

South Dakota Forms (continued)

9. The right, if given, of the remaining members of the limited liability company to continue the business on the death, retirement, resignation, expulsion, bankruptcy or dissolution of a member or occurrence of any other event which terminates the continued membership of a member in the limited liability company:

_____

_____

_____

_____

COMPLETE EITHER NUMBER TEN OR ELEVEN

10. If the limited liability company is to be managed by a manager or managers, state the names and addresses of the manager or managers who are to serve as managers until the first annual meeting of members or until their successors are elected and qualify:

_____

_____

_____

_____

11. If the management of a limited liability company is reserved to the members, the names and addresses of the members are:

_____

_____

_____

_____

12. Any other provisions, not inconsistent with law, which the members elect to set out in the articles of organization for the regulation of the internal affairs of the limited liability company:

_____

_____

_____

_____

Two or more members must sign in the presence of a notary public.   Date_____

_____   _____

_____   _____

STATE OF_____

COUNTY OF_____   ss

I,_____, a notary public, do hereby certify that on this_____day

of_____19_____, personally appeared before me_____

who, being by me first duly sworn, declared that he/she is the_____of

_____that he/she signed the foregoing document as

_____of the limited liability company and the statements therein contained are true.

My Commission Expires_____   _____

        (Notarial Seal)   Notary Public

South Dakota Forms (continued)

The Consent of Appointment below must be signed by the registered agent

---

CONSENT OF APPOINTMENT BY THE REGISTERED AGENT

I, _____, hereby give my consent to serve as the
(name of registered agent)

registered agent for _____
(limited liability company)

Dated _____ 19 _____   _____
(signature of registered agent)

Fee Schedule

* The filing fee must accompany the articles for filing. Make check payable to the
Secretary of State.

Filing articles of organization and issuing certificate of organization, if the initial capital
of the limited liability company is:

Not in excess of $50,000	$50
50,001 to 100,000	$100
in excess of $100,000	$100 for first $100,000 plus
	$ .50 for each additional $1,000

Filing Instructions

* Two or more persons who shall be members upon the issuance of the certificate
of organization may form a limited liability company.

* The words, "limited liability company" or the abbreviation "L.L.C." shall be the last
words of the name of every limited liability company.

* The period of duration may not exceed thirty years from the date of filing with the
secretary of state.

* A registered agent and registered office must be continuously maintained in this
state. Failure to continuously maintain a registered agent, or to contact the secretary
of state's office within thirty days of a change in registered agent and/or address,
will result in the forfeit of the certificate of organization.

* Sumit one original and one exact copy or photocopy of the articles of organization.

* AN ANNUAL TAX OF FIFTY DOLLARS ($50) IS DUE AND PAYABLE EACH JANUARY
2ND. A PENALTY FEE OF AN ADDITIONAL $50 SHALL BE ASSESSED IF NOT PAID
BY FEBRUARY FIRST.

Tennessee Forms

State of Tennessee

Department of State
Corporation Section

TENNESSEE ARTICLES OF ORGANIZATION OF A LIMITED LIABILITY COMPANY

For Office Use Only

The undersigned acting as organizer(s) of a Limited Liability Company under the provisions of the Tennessee Limited Liability Company Act, § 48A–5–101, adopts the following Articles of Organization.

1. The name of the Limited Liability Company is:

_____

(NOTE: Pursuant to the provisions of § 48A–7–101, each limited Liability Company name must contain the words "Limited Liability Company" or the abbreviation "LLC" or "L.L.C.")

2. The name and address of the Limited Liability Company's initial registered office in Tennessee is:

_____
(Name)

_____
(Street Address)   (City)   (State/Zip Code)

_____
(County)

3. List the name and address of the members organizing and/or members in this Limited Liability Company.

_____
(Name)   (Address: Include City, State and Zip Code)

_____
(Name)   (Address: Include City, State and Zip Code)

_____
(Name)   (Address: Include City, State and Zip Code)

4. At the date and time of formation there are two (2) or more members. Number of members _____.

5. The Limited Liability Company will be: (NOTE: PLEASE MARK APPLICABLE BOX)
    ☐ Board Managed   ☐ Member Managed

6. Number of members at the date of filing _____.

7. If the document is not to be effective upon filing by the Secretary of State, the delayed effective date and time is:
    Date _____, 19 _____ , Time _____

8. The complete address of the Limited Liability Company's principal office is:

_____
(Street Address)   (City)   (State/Country/Zip Code)

9. ☐ The Limited Liability Company has the power to expel a member.
    ☐ The Limited Liability Company does not have the power to expel a member.
    (NOTE: PLEASE MARK THE APPLICABLE BOX)

10. Period of Duration:

11. Other Provisions:

12. Do the members, parties (other than the LLC) to a contribution agreement or a contribution allowance agreement, have preemptive rights? (NOTE: PLEASE MARK THE APPLICABLE BOX)
    ☐ Yes   ☐ No

_____
Signature Date

_____
Signature (manager or member authorized to sign by the Limited Liability Company)

_____
Signer's Capacity

_____
Name (typed or printed)

SS-4249   RDA Pending

Tennessee Forms (continued)

State of Tennessee

Department of State
Corporations Section

CERTIFICATE OF FORMATION

For Office Use Only

Pursuant to the provisions of §48A-3-102 of the Tennessee Limited Liability Act, the undersigned hereby submits the following statement.

1. The Limited Liability Company was formed and the date of formation is _____.
(month, day and year)

2. At the date of formation the Limited Liability Company had two (2) or more members.

_____
Signature Date

_____
Signer's Capacity

_____
Name of Limited Liability Company

_____
Signature

_____
Name (typed or printed)

SS-4232

RDA Pending

Texas Form

[SPECIMEN FORM NOT TO BE USED FOR FILING]

> **CAVEAT**: Counsel will note that the Texas Limited Liability Company Act provides both for *articles of organization*, which is filed with the Texas Secretary of State, and for *regulations* which need not be filed with the Secretary of State. Inasmuch as the regulations would apparently have to be drafted *ad hoc* for each limited liability company, it is recommended that Counsel examine the provisions of the Texas Limited Liability Company Act prior to drafting both these documents.

ARTICLES OF ORGANIZATION

OF

_____

      FIRST: The name of the limited liability company (the "limited liability company") is

      SECOND: The period of duration of the limited liability company [shall expire on   , 19] [shall be perpetual].

      THIRD: The purpose for which the limited liability company is organized, which shall include the authority of the limited liability company to transact any lawful business, is

      FOURTH: The address of the registered office of the limited liability company in the State of Texas is   , and the name of the registered agent of the limited liability company at that address is

[Adapt one of the following for Article FIFTH]

TX LL D-:ART OF ORG 05/94-1

Texas Form (continued)

FIFTH: The limited liability company is to have [a manager] [managers]. The name and the address of the initial manager[s] of the limited liability company are as follows:

NAME   ADDRESS

FIFTH: The limited liability company will not have managers. The name and the address of the initial member[s] of the limited liability company are as follows:

NAME   ADDRESS

SIXTH: The name and the address of each organizer of the limited liability company are as follows:

NAME   ADDRESS

Signed on   , 19

_____
                                   , organizer

TX LL D-:ART OF ORG 05/94-2

Utah Form

State of Utah
DEPARTMENT OF COMMERCE
Division of Corporations & Commercial Code

Information on Filing
Articles of Organization for a
Limited Liability Company

A limited liability company ("the company") is formed in Utah by filing "Articles of Organization" with the Division of Corporations and Commercial Code, together with the filing fee of $75.00. While forms are not furnished for this purpose, the following information may be helpful to you. You are encouraged to consult an attorney to ensure your fullest legal protection and benefit.

1. Articles of Organization <u>must</u> include the following information:

   A. The name of the limited liability company (must contain the words "Limited Liability Company," "Limited Company," or "L.C.").
   B. The term of the company's existence.
   C. The specific purpose for which the company is formed. A company may engage in multiple activities.
   D. The name and Utah street address of the company's registered agent and office. You are encouraged to indicate the company's principal place of business, as well.
   E. The names and street addresses of the persons designated to be the management of the company. These names will be the managers, if the company is managed by managers, or these names will be the members, if the company is managed by its members.
   F. The signature of at least two members or managers, and the signature of the registered agent acknowledging appointment as such.

2. When filing Articles of Organization, you <u>must</u> submit the following:

   A. One (1) executed original of the Articles of Organization and one (1) copy of the original containing all of the information listed above.
   B. The filing fee of $75.00 payable to the State of Utah.

Vermont Form

VERMONT SECRETARY OF STATE

LIMITED LIABILITY COMPANY ARTICLES OF ORGANIZATION

Name of LLC: _____
(Name must contain the words Limited Liability Company, Limited Company, LLC, LC; limited may be abbrev as Ltd and Company as Co.)

Organized under the laws of the state (or country) of : _____

A Foreign LLC (non VT) must attach a good standing certificate, dated no earlier than 30 days prior to filing, from its state of origin.

Address of principal office: _____ *City* _____ *State* ____ *Zip* _____

Name of process agent: Corporation Service Company _____

Agents address: 159 State Street _____ *City* Montpelier _____ **VT** ____ *Zip* 05602 ____

An agent is the person or "corporation", residing IN Vt, who is authorized to receive service of process. An LLC cannot be an agent.

The fiscal year ends the month of _____ . *(DEC will be designated as the month your year ends unless you state differently.)*

Is the company a TERM Limited Liability Company? _____ if YES, state the duration of its term: _____
(An LLC is an At-Will Company unless it is designated in its articles of organization as a Term Company)

This is a MANAGER-MANAGED company. [ ] YES [ ] NO

If the LLC is Manager-Managed list the name and address of each initial MANAGER:

_____

_____

_____

Indicate below whether the member of the company are to be personally liable for its debts and obligations under

11 VSA, 3043(b): _____

List name and address of each organizer: _____

_____

SIGNATURE OF ORGANIZER(S): _____

The articles must be typewritten or printed and filed in duplicate. Unless a delayed effective date is specified, the document is effective on the date it is approved. A delayed effective date cannot be later than the 90th day after filing.
ANNUAL REPORT: Each LLC under this title is required to file an annual report within 2-1/2 months of the close of its fiscal year end. Failure to file this report will result in termination of the LLC. The annual report form will be mailed to your process agent when the report is due.

FEES: VERMONT DOMESTIC LLC = $75.00   FOREIGN LLC = $100.00

Virginia Form

LLC-1011 (8/95)

COMMONWEALTH OF VIRGINIA
STATE CORPORATION COMMISSION
ARTICLES OF ORGANIZATION

Pursuant to Chapter 12 of Title 13.1 of the Code of Virginia the
undersigned states as follows:

1. The name of the limited liability company is

    _____.

    (The name must contain the words "limited company" or "limited
    liability company" or their abbreviations "L.C.", "LC",
    "L.L.C." OR "LLC")

2. The address of the initial registered office in Virginia is

    _____,

    (number/street)   (city/state/zip)

    located in the [X] city or [ ] county of _____.

3. A. The registered agent's name is _____
    whose business address is identical with the registered office.

    B. The registered agent is (mark appropriate box)
       (1) an INDIVIDUAL who is a resident of Virginia and
           [ ] a member/manager of the limited liability company
           [ ] an officer/director of a corporate member/manager
               of the limited liability company
           [ ] a general partner of a general or limited partnership
               member/manager of the limited liability company
           [ ] a member of the Virginia State Bar
                              OR
       (2) [ ] a professional corporation or a professional limited
               liability company of attorneys registered under
               Virginia Code § 54.1-3902

4. The post office address of the principal office where the records
    will be maintained pursuant to Virginia Code § 13.1-1028 is

    _____.

    (number/street)   (city/state/zip)

5. The latest date on which the limited liability company is to
    be dissolved and its affairs wound up is

    _____.

6. Signature:

    _____   _____
          (organizer)   (date)

    _____
         (printed name)

              SEE INSTRUCTIONS ON THE REVERSE

Virginia Form (continued)

INSTRUCTIONS

The registered office must include the complete post office address, including a street address, if any, or a rural route and box number. Also, state the name of the city or county in which the office is physically located. Cities and counties in Virginia are separate local jurisdictions.

The document can be executed in the name of the limited liability company by any person (see Virginia Code §§ 13.1-603 and 13.1-1003).

Submit the original articles to the Clerk of the Commission.

Virginia Code § 13.1-1003 requires that this document be type-written or printed in black.

Washington Forms

SECRETARY
of STATE

CERTIFICATE OF FORMATION FOR A
LIMITED LIABILITY COMPANY
RCW 25.15.070

UBI #: _____

Phone #: _____

Pursuant to RCW 25.15.070 of the Revised Code of Washington, the undersigned does hereby submit this Certificate of Formation for Limited Liability Company.

1. The name of the Limited Liability Company is: _____

    _____

    (Name shown above must contain the either the words "Limited Liability Company," "Limited Liability Co.," or "L.L.C.".)

2. The latest date on which the Limited Liability Company is to dissolve is: _____

3. The address of the principal place of business of the Limited Liability Company is:

    Number and Street_____

    City_____ WA Zip Code _____

4. The name of the registered agent is: _____
    (The registered agent must reside in the state of Washington and sign the consent to appointment as registered agent)

4a. The registered office, which address is identical to the business office of the registered agent in Washington, is:

    Number and Street_____

    City_____ WA Zip Code _____

4b. (Optional) The post office box address, located in the same city as the Washington registered office address, which may be used for mailing purposes only, is:

    PO Box _____ City _____ WA Zip Code _____

5. **CONSENT TO APPOINTMENT AS REGISTERED AGENT**

    I, _____, hereby consent to serve as Registered Agent in the State of Washington for the above named Limited Liability Company. I understand that as agent for the Limited Liability Company, it will be my responsibility to accept Service of Process on behalf of the Limited Liability Company; to forward mail to the Limited Liability Company; and to immediately notify the Office of the Secretary of State in the event of my resignation or of any changes in the Registered Office address.

X By: _____   _____ _____

    (Signature of Registered Agent)   Print Name and Title)   (Date)

025-001 (1/96)

Washington Forms (continued)

6. Management of the limited liability company is vested in one or more members/managers:
☐ **Yes** ☐ **No**

7. **Attach copy of any other provisions the limited liability company elects to include.**

8. The name and address of each member/manager executing this certificate is:

Name	Address	City	State	Zip Code

9. This application will be effective upon filing unless a date and/or time is specified: _____
   (Note: Extended effective date may not be set at not more than 90 days beyond the date the document is stamped "Filed" by the Secretary of State.)

10. This document is hereby executed under penalties of perjury, and is, to the best of my knowledge true and correct.
    Dated: _____, 19_____.

X _____   _____
    (Signature)   (Type or Print Name)

X _____   _____
    (Signature)   (Type or Print Name)

X _____   _____
    (Signature)   (Type or Print Name)

X _____   _____
    (Signature)   (Type or Print Name)

X _____   _____
    (Signature)   (Type or Print Name)

X _____   _____
    (Signature)   (Type or Print Name)

025-001 (1/96)

Washington Forms (continued)

SECRETARY of STATE

CERTIFICATE OF FORMATION FOR A
LIMITED LIABILITY COMPANY
RCW 25.15.070
(Copies of the RCW law may be obtained at local and state libraries.)

CHECK LIST
All documents must be typewritten or printed legibly in ink.

- [ ] 1. Limited Liability Company name must be available for use and contain a Limited Liability Company designation which may be "Limited Liability Company," "Limited Liability Co.," or "L.L.C.". (A name may be reserved in advanced and held for a period of 180 days. Reservation fee is $30.00)

- [ ] 2. The latest date on which the Limited Liability Company is to dissolve

- [ ] 3. Street address of principal place of business for Limited Liability Company.

- [ ] 4. The registered agent must be a resident of the state of Washington or a current corporation registered in Washington.

- [ ] 4a. The registered office address must have a physical street address identical to the business address of the registered agent.

- [ ] 4b. **OPTIONAL** - If you choose to use a post office box, a street address within the same city is required.

- [ ] 5. The registered agent must sign the consent to appointment.

- [ ] 6. Select appropriate box if the L.L.C. is vested in one or more managers/members.

- [ ] 7. **Attach copy of any other provisions the limited liability company elects to include.**

- [ ] 8. The name(s) and addressees) of each person executing the certificate must be listed.

- [ ] 9. The application will be effective upon filing, unless an extended date or time is selected.

- [ ] 10. This document is to be signed by manager/member.

PAYMENT REQUIREMENTS

- [ ] The required fee of **$175.00** must accompany the application. (Make check payable to **Secretary of State.**)

025-001 (1/96)

Washington Forms (continued)

EXPEDITED SERVICE
The filing fee plus $20.00 must be included for expedited service.

For immediate assistance you can come to the Corporations Division office to have your document(s) filed while you wait.

You can also receive this service through the mail by marking **EXPEDITE** in bold letters on the outside of the envelope. Please include a cover letter stating a day-time telephone number and contact that can be reached for any questions we may have. Requests will be processed and mailed within 24 hours.

<u>**Please Note:**</u> If this Limited Liability Company has been issued an **UBI** (Unified Business Identifier) number, under the name shown in this document, by any Washington State agency, **LIST** that number at the top of the application in the space provided.

IMPORTANT NOTICE

Within 120 days after filing the Certificate of Formation, an **INITIAL REPORT** <u>must</u> be filed with the Office of the Secretary of State. The **INITIAL REPORT** will be sent to the registered agent at the registered office address within four weeks of the file date. The Limited Liability Company <u>must</u> request replacement forms if they do not receive the **INITIAL REPORT** form. To avoid dissolution/termination of your Limited Liability Company status, complete and return the **INITIAL REPORT** and the **$10.00** filing fee within the time frame indicated.

025-001 (1/96)

West Virginia Form

KEN HECHLER
Secretary of State
State Capitol, W-139
Charleston, WV 25305-0770
(304) 342-8000

FILE IN DUPLICATE
ORIGINALS FEE: $10.00

West Virginia Articles of Organization
of a Limited Liability Company

The undersigned, acting as organizer(s)of a limited liability company under Chapter 31, Article 1A, of the West Virginia Code, adopt(s) the following Articles of Organization.

1. The undersigned agree to become a West Virginia limited liability company by the name of

_____(The name of the corporation shall contain the words: Limited Liability Company, without abbreviation)

2. The address of the principal office will be _____
_____ street, in the city, town or
village of _____, county of _____
State of _____, Zip code_____
3. Purpose of organization: _____
_____
_____
4. Name and address of the initial registered agent for service of process.

Name _____
Address, Street or P.O. Box _____
City _____, State _____, Zip _____
5. List the name and addresses of the members organizing and/or members in this limited liability company: (NOTE: Foreign corporations must also apply for a certificate of authority)
        Name   Address

_____   _____
_____   _____
_____   _____
_____   _____(attach
additional sheets if necessary)

_____
        Manager or member authorized to sign by the limited liability Co.
Form I-LLL

West Virginia Form (continued)

Acknowledgement

═══

I(We), the understand, for the purpose of organizing a limited liability company under the laws of the laws of the State of West Virginia, do make and file this "Articles of organization"

In witness whereof, I(We)have accordingly hereunto set my(our) respective hands this _____day of _____, 19_____.

(All organizers must sign below. Names and signatures must appear the same throughout the Articles of organization).
PHOTOCOPIES OF THE SIGNATURES OF THE ORGANIZERS AND THE NOTARY PUBLIC CANNOT BE ACCEPTED.

_____

_____   _____

State of _____

County of _____

I, _____, a Notary Public, in and for the county and state aforesaid, hereby certify that (names of all organizer(s) as shown above must be inserted in this space by official taking acknowledgement)

_____

_____   _____

whose name(s) is(are) signed to the foregoing Articles of organization, this day personally appeared before me in my said county and acknowledged his(her)(their) signature(s).

_____ My

commission expires

_____
SEAL   (Notary Public)

Articles of organization prepared by _____
whose mailing address is _____

Wisconsin Form

ARTICLES OF ORGANIZATION
Limited Liability Company
(Organized under Chapter 183 of the Wisconsin Statutes)

⌐

Please indicate where you would
like the acknowledgement copy of
the filed document sent. Please
include complete name and mailing
address.

∟

Your phone number during the day: (_____) _____ - _____

INSTRUCTIONS (Ref. s.180.0202 Wis. Stats. for document content)

Submit one original and one exact copy to DEPT. OF FINANCIAL INSTITUTIONS, P O Box 7846, Madison WI, 53707-7846. (If sent by Express or Priority US mail, address to 30 W. Mifflin St., 9th Floor, Madison WI, 53703.) The original must bear an original, manual signature, per sec. 183.0107(2), Stats. If you have questions, please contact the Corporations unit at (608) 266-3590.

<u>Article 1.</u> The name must contain the words "Limited Liability Company" or "Limited Liability Co." or end with the abbreviation "L.L.C." or "LLC". If you wish to provide a second choice name that you would accept if your first choice is not available, indicate it here: _____

<u>Articles 2 & 3.</u> The organization must have a registered agent located at a registered office in Wisconsin. The address of the registered office must be a physical location. State street number and name, city and ZIP code in Wisconsin. P.O. Box addresses may be included as part of the address, but are insufficient alone. The organization may not name itself as registered agent.

<u>Article 4.</u> Indicate whether the management of the limited liability company will be vested in a manager or managers, or in its members. Select only one choice. (Ref. s.183.0401(2), Wis. Stats.)

<u>Article 5.</u> All persons organizing the limited liability company must sign the document and print or typewrite name and complete address. Only one organizer is required.

If the document is executed in Wisconsin, s. 182.01(3), Stats., provides that it shall not be filed unless the name of the drafter (either an individual or a governmental agency) is printed in a legible manner. If the document is NOT executed in Wisconsin, please so state.

Subject to the conditions set in ss. 183.0110 and 183.0111, Stats., the organization's existence commences on the date that acceptable articles of organization are received by the Department of Financial Institutions, unless a delayed (future) effective date is declared in the document. To name a delayed effective date, enter a remark "This document has a delayed effective date of (enter the future date).". The delayed effective date may not be more than 90 days after the date the document is received by the department for filing.

NOTE: This document sets forth the required and exclusive contents of articles of organization of a limited liability company. Articles of organization not containing all the required information, or containing additional information, will be rejected by the department as not being in compliance with sec. 183.0202, Stats. Non-required information may be set forth in an operating agreement.

When the document has been filed by the Department of Financial Institutions, an acknowledgement copy stamped "FILED" will be sent to the address indicated above.

<u>FILING FEE</u>
$130.00. Submit document with check payable to DEPARTMENT OF FINANCIAL INSTITUTIONS.

Wisconsin Form (continued)

DFI/CCS/Corp
Form 502
WISCONSIN
(7/96)

ARTICLES OF ORGANIZATION
Limited Liability Company
(Organized under Chapter 183 of the Wisconsin Statutes)

Executed by the undersigned for the purpose of forming a Wisconsin
Limited Liability Company under Chapter 183 of the Wisconsin Statutes:

Article 1. (See instruction 1 for required words or abbreviations.)

    Name of Limited Liability Company: _____

Article 2. The street address of the initial registered office is:
    (The complete address, including street and number, if
    assigned, and ZIP code. P.O. Box address may be
    included as part of the address, but is insufficient alone.)

Article 3. The name of the initial registered agent at the above registered office is:

_____

Article 4. Select appropriate choice below. (See information on reverse.)
    Management of the limited liability company shall be vested in:

    ( ) a manager or managers.
  OR
    ( ) its members.

Article 5. Date executed _____.

    <u>Name</u> and <u>complete address</u> of each organizer:
    1)   2)

_____   _____
    (Organizer's Signature)   *(Organizer's Signature)*

This document was drafted by _____
                             (name of individual is required by law)

FILING FEE - $130
<u>SEE REVERSE</u> for Instructions, Suggestions, Filing Fees and Procedures

Printed on Recycled Paper

Wyoming Form

[SPECIMEN FORM NOT TO BE USED FOR FILING]

CAVEAT: Counsel will note that the Wyoming Limited Liability Company Act provides both for *articles of organization*, which is filed with the Wyoming Secretary of State, and for an *operating agreement* which need not be filed with the Secretary of State. Inasmuch as an operating agreement would apparently have to be drafted *ad hoc* for each limited liability company, it is recommended that Counsel examine the provisions of the Wyoming Limited Liability Company Act prior to drafting both these documents. The annexed CSC brochure WYOMING - LIMITED LIABILITY COMPANY - FORMATION is intended to assist Counsel in this research.

ARTICLES OF ORGANIZATION

OF

_____

The undersigned individuals, for the purpose of organizing a limited liability company pursuant to the provisions of the Wyoming Limited Liability Company Act, do hereby adopt the following Articles of Organization.

FIRST: The name of the limited liability company (hereinafter called the "limited liability company") is:

SECOND: The period of the duration of the limited liability company shall expire on

THIRD: The purpose for which the limited liability company is organized is as follows:

FOURTH: The name and the address of the registered agent of the limited liability company in the State of Wyoming are: Corporation Service Company, 1821 Logan Avenue, Cheyenne, Wyoming 82001.

FIFTH: The total amount of cash contributed to the limited liability company is:

Wyoming Form (continued)

SIXTH: A description of property other than cash contributed to the limited liability company and the agreed value thereof are as follows:

DESCRIPTION:

AGREED VALUE:

SEVENTH: The total additional contributions, if any, agreed to be made by all members to the limited liability company, and the times at which or the events upon the happening of which they shall be made, are as follows:

[Take or adapt one the following for Article EIGHTH]

EIGHTH: The members of the limited liability company shall have the right to admit other members to the limited liability company. The terms and the conditions of the said admission are as follows:

EIGHTH: The members of the limited liability company shall not have the right to admit other members to the limited liability company.

NINTH: On the death, retirement, resignation, expulsion, bankruptcy, or dissolution of a member, or on the occurrence of any other event which terminates the continued membership of a member in the limited liability company, the remaining members of the limited liability company shall [not] have the right to continue the business of the limited liability company.

[Adapt one of the following for Article TENTH]

TENTH: The limited liability company is to be managed by a manager or managers. The name and the address of each manager who is to serve as a manager until the first annual meeting of members or until the said manager's successor is elected and qualifies are as follows:

NAME   ADDRESS

WY LL D-:ARTICLES OF ORGANIZATION 08/96-2 (#627)

Wyoming Form (continued)

TENTH: The management of the limited liability company is reserved to the members of the limited liability company. The name and the address of each of the aforesaid members are as follows:

NAME   ADDRESS

Signed on   , 19

_____
[name]

_____
[name]

Secretary of State
State of Wyoming

CONSENT TO APPOINTMENT BY REGISTERED AGENT

1. The Corporation Service Company, voluntarily consents to serve as the registered agent for   on the date shown below.

2. The registered agent certifies that it is a foreign corporation authorized to transact business in this state whose business office is identical with the registered office.

3. The registered agent knows and understands the duties of a registered agent as set forth in the Wyoming Limited Liability Company Act.

Date   , 19

Corporation Service Company

By: _____
Signature of Registered Agent

WY LL D-:ARTICLES OF ORGANIZATION 08/96-3 (#627)

Glossary

ACCRUAL METHOD — The method of accounting where income and expenses are recognized when they arise, and not necessarily when they are received or paid.

ACQUISITION — Obtaining control of another corporation or LLC by purchasing all or a majority of its outstanding stock or by purchasing its assets.

AMENDMENT — Change of existing provisions of the articles of incorporation or articles of formation (LLC) of a domestic corporation or an LLC.

ANNUAL MEETING — A yearly meeting of shareholders of a corporation or members of a limited liability company.

ANNUAL REPORT — A required annual filing in a state, usually listing directors (or members if an LLC), officers, and financial information. Also, an annual statement of business and affairs of the company to interested parties.

ARTICLES OF ORGANIZATION — The name of the document filed in most states to create a limited liability company or corporation.

AT–RISK AMOUNT — Generally, the amount of an owner's cash contribution, plus the tax basis of assets contributed, plus amounts borrowed for use in the activity if the owner has personal liability for the borrowed amounts.

BOND — A long term debt security secured by a mortgage on real property or a lien on other fixed assets.

CASH METHOD — The method of accounting where all income is recognized only when it is received and expenses are recognized only when they are disbursed.

CLOSE CORPORATION — A close corporation has less than 50 shareholders and elects in its articles of incorporation to be treated as a close corporation. Close corporations can eliminate or limit the powers of the board of directors, and corporate formality requirements are relaxed. Not all states recognize close corporations.

CONTINUITY OF LIFE — Even if the death, mental breakdown, bankruptcy, retirement, resignation, or expulsion of any stockholder occurs within the corporation, the life of the corporation will be perpetual unless a certificate of dissolution is filed within the state of the entity in question.

DISSOLUTION — The statutory procedure which terminates the existence of a corporation or an LLC.

DISTRIBUTION — A transfer of money or other property made by a corporation or an LLC to a shareholder or member.

DIVIDEND — A distribution of the earnings of a corporation to its shareholders.

DOUBLE TAX TREATY — Agreement between countries to prevent double taxation of individuals working in a foreign country from their citizenship.

DOUBLE TAXATION — Taxing the same item or piece of property twice to the same person.

FOREIGN CORPORATION — A term applied to a corporation conducting business in a state other than its state of incorporation.

FOREIGN LIMITED LIABILITY COMPANY — A term applied to a limited liability company conducting business in a state other than its state of formation.

FRANCHISE TAX — A privilege tax levied upon a corporation's or an LLC's right to exist or to conduct business in a particular state.

GENERAL CORPORATION — An artificial entity created under and governed by the laws of its state of incorporation.

GENERAL PARTNER — A partner in a general or in a limited partnership who has the right to participate in management of the partnership and who assumes personal liability for partnership obligations.

GENERAL PARTNERSHIP — An unincorporated organization having at least two owners, none of which is a limited partner, that carries on any business or venture, and that is not a trust, estate, or corporation.

HOLDING COMPANY — A corporate entity that generates passive income outside its state of incorporation.

INCORPORATION — The act of creating or organizing a corporation.

INDEMNIFICATION — Financial or other protection provided by a corporation or an LLC to its directors, members (LLC), officers, and employees. This protects them against expenses and liabilities incurred by them in lawsuits that allege they breached some duty in their service to or on the behalf of the corporation.

INVOLUNTARY DISSOLUTION — The termination of a corporation's or an LLC's existence pursuant to an administrative or judicial proceeding. This dissolution is forced upon a corporation or an LLC rather than decided upon at the initiative of the corporation or limited liability company.

JOINT VENTURE — A form of business organization similar to a partnership.

JUDICIAL DISSOLUTION — Involuntary dissolution of a corporation or an LLC by a court at the request of the state attorney general, a shareholder, a member (LLC), or a creditor.

LIMITED LIABILITY COMPANY (LLC) — An artificial entity created under and governed by the laws of its state of formation.

LIMITED PARTNER — A partner whose liability to third party creditors of the partnership is limited to that amount invested by such partner in the partnership.

LIMITED PARTNERSHIP — A statutory form of partnership consisting of general partner(s) who manage the business and are liable for its debts, and limited partner(s) who invest in the business and have limited liability for the business debt.

LIMITED PERSONAL LIABILITY — The protection generally afforded a corporate shareholder, limited partner, or an LLC member from the debts of and claims against the company.

MAJORITY — Fifty percent plus one. Commonly used as the percentage of votes required to approve corporate or LLC actions.

MANAGEMENT — The board of directors of a corporation; the members of the limited liability company; the executive officers of the company.

MANAGER — The individual(s) who, as a group known as the board of directors, manage the affairs of the limited liability company.

MEMBER — The owner(s) of a limited liability company. Most states require at least two members who act in a similar fashion as the board of directors of a corporation.

MEMBERSHIP CERTIFICATE — Tangible evidence of a member's ownership of a limited liability company.

MERGER — The statutory combination of two or more corporations or limited liability companies in which one entity survives and the other ceases to exist. Also, the method whereby a corporation can transform into a limited liability company.

NAME RESERVATION — A procedure that allows those forming a corporation or a limited liability company to obtain exclusive use of the name for a specified period of time to form a company.

OPERATING AGREEMENT — A contract among LLC members governing the management, operation, and distribution of income of the LLC.

OPERATING PARTNER — Another term for a general partner in a limited partnership.

ORGANIZATIONAL MEETING — Meeting of initial directors or members held after filing the articles of incorporation or formation (LLC) in order to complete the organization of the company.

PARTNERSHIP — A form of business organization in which two or more persons agree to conduct business together.

PARTNERSHIP AGREEMENT — A document embodying the terms and conditions of a partnership and sometimes referred to as the articles of partnership.

PASS-THROUGH TAX TREATMENT — The tax treatment generally afforded an S corporation, partnership, or LLC whereby no income tax is paid at the entity level. Instead, the income of the entity is passed through to its owners and taxed on their individual tax returns.

PASSIVE ACTIVITY — Any trade or business in which the taxpayer does not materially participate and/or any rental activity.

PASSIVE ACTIVITY LOSS RESTRICTIONS — Prevents LLC members from deducting passive activity losses to the extent that the losses exceed the members' income from passive activities.

REGISTERED AGENT — An agent required to be appointed by a corporation or an LLC whose authority is limited to receiving legal process issued against a corporation. Also known as Agent for Service of Process.

S CORPORATION — An S corporation is created under the Internal Revenue Code. It prevents double taxation by passing through all profits or losses from the business directly to the stockholders' personal income tax return. A corporation may elect to be an S corporation. Stringent rules exist with respect to how and when the election is made, the number and type of shareholders, and the means by which the election may be terminated.

SOLE PROPRIETORSHIP — A one-owner, unincorporated business in which the owner is personally liable for all business debt and claims against the business.

STOCK — Represents ownership in the corporation and is often evidenced by a stock certificate.

STOCKHOLDERS — Individuals who own the issued stock of a corporation. They do not own specific corporate property of the corporation, but own an interest in the entire corporation.

SUBSIDIARY — A company wholly controlled by another.

TAX BASIS OF AN ASSET — Generally, the original cost of the asset less depreciation deductions allowed with respect to the asset.

TAX SHELTER — Any legal means within the purview of the Internal Revenue Code with methods of legitimate tax avoidance.

VENTURE CAPITAL — Invested funds with high risk, with the aim of making money.

VOLUNTARY DISSOLUTION — Action by shareholder or directors in corporations, or members in LLCs to voluntarily dissolve a corporation or an LLC.

Index

L

From The Leading Publisher of Small Business Information
Books that save you time and money.

If you ever wondered how to combine business success and personal significance, author Gerald Baron has numerous practical suggestions. After years of working with executives and entrepreneurs, he's found that business success and personal meaning can share common ground. Using dozens of real-life examples, he shows how building relationships is the key to business development and fulfillment.

Friendship Marketing   **Pages: 187**
Paperback: $18.95   ISBN: 1-55571-399-8

Learn to capitalize on your customers' feelings of satisfaction with your product and your business. Thirty-one comprehensive worksheets outline a successful marketing approach for your business. Marketing is presented in a seven step process that will help you acquire and keep satisfied customers.

Marketing Mastery   **Pages: 268**
Paperback: $19.95   ISBN: 1-55571-357-2
Binder: $39.95   ISBN: 1-55571-358-0

In business, the banker or the institution that they represent are often perceived as opponents to your business' success. Shows why business owners should take a leading role in developing and nurturing a worthwhile and lasting partnership with their banker. This inside look will help new, as well as seasoned business owners develop a functional understanding of how the banking industry operates, how to speak their language, and how to turn your banker into an advocate for the growth and success of your small business.

The Small Business Insider's Guide to Bankers   **Pages: 176**
Paperback: $18.95   ISBN: 1-55571-400-5

Guides the inventive spirit through all the stages of new product development. Discusses patenting your invention, trademarks, copyrights, and how to construct your prototype. Provides valuable information on financing, distribution test marketing, and finding licensees. Plus, lists many useful sources of prototype resources, trade shows, funding, and more.

Develop & Market Your Creative Ideas   **Pages: 208**
Paperback: $15.95   ISBN: 1-55571-383-1

From The Leading Publisher of Small Business Information
Books that save you time and money.

Pursuing a high-tech business has never been more opportune, however the competition in the industry is downright grueling. Author Richard Manweller brings a smart, in-depth strategy with motivational meaning. It will show you how to tailor your strategy to gain investor's attention. If you are looking for a financial angel, *Funding High Tech Ventures* is the guidance your need to make the right match.

Funding High-Tech Ventures   **Pages: 160**
Paperback: $21.95   ISBN: 1-55571-405-6

BusinessBasics clearly illustrates the starting skills small business owners need to nurture a prosperous business. It covers five unique aspects of essential administrative skills in one comprehensive and enjoyable workbook. Several exercises and worksheets will help you build stronger management and business skills.

BusinessBasics: A Microbusiness Startup Guide   Pages: 235
Paperback: $17.95   ISBN: 1-55571-430-7

Essential for the small business operator in search of capital, this helpful, hands-on guide simplifies the loan application process as never before. The Insider's Guide to Small Business Loans is an easy-to-follow road map designed to help you cut through the red tape and show you how to prepare a successful loan application. Several chapters are devoted to helping you secure a loan guaranty from the Small Business Administration.

The Insider's Guide to Small Business Loans   Pages: 200
Paperback: $19.95   ISBN: 1-55571-429-3
Binder: $29.95   ISBN: 1-55571-378-5

Anyone who has ever listened to a banker and not understood a word will do well to read this guide. It explains the basic principles of finance, from realizing that business is all about making the most money possible with the least investment to understanding cash flow. Learn how to analyze financial statements, how debt is used to a business' advantage, and how to understand stock pricing. Business segment accounting, mergers and acquisitions, currency hedging, and incorporation, are outlined as well.

Financial Decisionmaking   **Pages: 230**
Paperback: $19.95   ISBN: 1-55571-435-8

From The Leading Publisher of Small Business Information
Books that save you time and money.

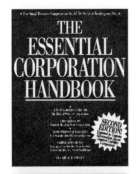

A comprehensive reference of the types of small business corporations no matter where you are located in the United States. It explains the legal requirements for maintaining a corporation in good standing. Features sample corporate documents, which are annotated by the author to show what you should look for. Tells how to avoid personal liability as an officer, director, or shareholder.

The Essential Corporation Handbook   **Pages: 300**
Paperback: $21.95   **ISBN: 1-55571-421-8**

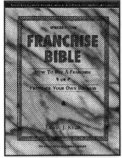

A franchise attorney developed this up-to-date guide for prospective franchisees or for those who want to franchise their own business. Includes sample documents, such as the latest FTC- approved offering circular, plus worksheets for evaluating franchise companies, locations, and organizing information before seeing an attorney. A valuable resource for lawyers as well as their clients.

Franchise Bible   **Pages: 300**
Paperback: $24.95   **ISBN: 1-55571-367-X**

Covers all the steps of planning, opening, and managing a retail store of your own, beginning with an honest assessment of whether you are really suited to running a business, Contains practical information on planning a store opening, from selecting a product line and hiring employees to buying an initial inventory and obtaining the required permits, licenses, and tax numbers. Real information you can apply to your retail business today.

Retail in Detail   **Pages: 168**
Paperback: $15.95   **ISBN: 1-55571-371-8**

Written for the business owner or manager who is not a personnel specialist. Explains what you must know to make your hiring decisions pay off for everyone. Learn more about the American with Disabilities Act (ADA), Medical and Family Leave, and more.

People Investment   **Pages: 224**
Paperback: $19.95   **ISBN: 1-55571-161-8**
Binder: $39.95   **ISBN: 1-55571-187-1**